even more themed intercessions

david adam

kevin
mayhew

First published in 2007 by

KEVIN MAYHEW LTD
Buxhall, Stowmarket, Suffolk, IP14 3BW
E-mail: info@kevinmayhewltd.com
Web: www.kevinmayhew.com

Even More Themed Intercessions is extracted from *Searchlights,* Complete Resource Book, Year A.

9 8 7 6 5 4 3 2 1 0

ISBN 978 1 84417 878 0
Catalogue No 1501059

Cover design by Sara-Jane Came
Typesetting by Richard Weaver

Printed in Great Britain

Contents

God's creation

God's kingdom

Seasons

Introduction

Intercession is a time when we should rejoice in the presence and power of God, knowing that his desire is for our well-being and good. God knows our needs and our concerns. He does not need to be informed by us but he does want us to share them with him. One of the wonderful things of intercession is to know we are not alone: God is at work and God cares for us.

As the themes of worship change from week to week, this should encourage us to be looking at new opportunities of prayer and praise and of intercession, as suggested by the themes. This book is meant to be a guide to help you do just that.

Let a variety of people lead the intercessions. Normally the weekly intercessions are divided up into prayers for the Church, the world, the home, the ill and needy, and finally the saints and the departed. A different person could be used for each group of prayers. Make sure the congregation can hear all who lead prayers. There is very little worse in worship than mumbled and indistinct voices, so encourage any would-be intercessors to practise. Remember to use different age groups; intercessions is a good time for some of the young people to lead part of the worship.

Encourage everyone to come to the Eucharist with something to give thanks for and someone or some event to pray for: with what used to be called 'a special intention'; that is, with someone on their heart to bring before God. Incorporate silences into the intercessions, where people have the opportunity to add their own prayers. Sometimes allow room for extempore intercession where members can pray aloud what is on their hearts. Have a prayer board within the church buildings where people can write out what they want to pray for, then use it in intercessions. Sometimes I have provided a plate like a collection plate where people can put their written intercessions. This is placed on the altar at the beginning of the service, and often left there all day. Whenever we make intercession we are sharing with our Lord who makes intercession for us.

David Adam

1 Seeing God's glory

Blessed are you, Lord God,
ever present in our lives.
Through the power of your Spirit
you reveal your glory to us
in the face of Jesus Christ.
Help us to trust in you
and in the power of the resurrection.
Blessed are you, Father, Son and Holy Spirit.

Lord, guide your Church,
that in its words and actions
it may reveal your glory.
We ask your blessing
upon preachers of the word
and ministers of the sacraments,
that they may help us to do your will
and to have a vision of your purpose,
and that each in our mission
may proclaim your kingdom and your glory.

Silence

God, in your goodness,
grant us a glimpse of your glory.

We remember all who have lost their way
and who feel confused by life,
especially those who feel life has no meaning or purpose.
We pray for all who are captives of vice or drugs.
We ask your blessing
upon all who are fearful,
especially those who are suffering
from persecution or poverty.

Silence

God, in your goodness,
grant us a glimpse of your glory.

Lord, change us and we shall be changed.
Transform our homes into places of your glory.
Transform our lives to reveal your presence.
Transform our minds to know your peace.
Transform our hearts to abide in your love.
May we know you are always with our loved ones
and with us.

Silence

God, in your goodness,
grant us a glimpse of your glory.

Lord, transform our darkness with your light.
We ask your blessing
upon all who are struggling with illness
or who are no longer able to cope on their own.
We pray for all who have been injured
in accidents or through violence this week.
We pray for the work of the rescue services
and all who seek to bring and maintain peace.

Silence

God, in your goodness,
grant us a glimpse of your glory.

We rejoice in your power
and in the resurrection.
We pray for friends and loved ones departed,
that they may enjoy and rest in your glory.
We seek to share in the fellowship
of all your saints in glory.

Silence

Merciful Father,
accept these prayers
for the sake of your Son,
our Saviour Jesus Christ.
Amen.

2 The Lord among us

Blessed are you, Lord our God,
for out of your love you have made all things.
You come to us and give yourself to us.
Help us to be aware of your love in our lives
and to give ourselves to you
in love and in doing your will.
Blessed are you, Father, Son and Holy Spirit.

Lord, as you abide in us,
let our lives show your love for all of your creation.
We remember all Christians
who are being persecuted for their faith
or have to suffer scorn and mockery
from those with whom they live.
We pray for all who witness to you
amid danger and opposition.
We ask your blessing upon all who are new to the faith.
We pray for those who have recently been converted
and for those who have been baptised and confirmed.

Silence

Lord of life,
be known to be among us.

Lord, we remember all places where people are suffering
from tyranny or lawlessness.
We pray for all who are oppressed or used as cheap labour.
We ask your blessing upon all who strive
for justice, freedom, peace and fair trade.

Silence

Lord of life,
be known to be among us.

Lord, may our homes reflect the love we share.
Keep us sensitive to the needs of each other.
May we be ready to take our share
in the work of our own home.

We remember before you
all who feel unloved and unwanted.
We ask your blessing
upon all homeless people and refugees.
We pray for all who are suffering
from broken relationships and broken trust.

Silence

Lord of life,
be known to be among us.

Lord of light, we ask your blessing
upon all who are struggling with darkness and fear.
We remember those who have been involved
in accidents or in acts of violence this week.
We pray for all who have suddenly become ill
and those who are in hospital.
We pray for all who anxiously await
the results of a medical examination.

Silence

Lord of life,
be known to be among us.

Lord of life,
we rejoice in the power of the resurrection
and we remember before you
all your saints and martyrs.
We ask your blessing upon our loved ones and benefactors
who have now departed from us.
May we all abide in your presence and eternal love.

Silence

Merciful Father,
accept these prayers
for the sake of your Son,
our Saviour Jesus Christ.
Amen.

3 Our guide on the journey

Blessed are you, Lord God,
for in your Son Jesus Christ
you have opened for us the way to glory.
In him the world is seen in greater depth
and in him is the gift of eternal life.
Lord, ease our troubled hearts
and help us to put our faith in you.
Blessed are you, Father, Son and Holy Spirit.

Lord God, teach us to walk in your way
and to rejoice in your truth,
that we may know the fullness of life eternal.
We ask your blessing upon all spiritual leaders,
preachers of the word and ministers of the sacraments.
We pray for all who are new to the faith
and all who are growing in a deeper awareness of your presence.
May we all know that wherever we go and whatever happens
you are with us and ready to lead us.

Silence

Lord, guide our journeying:
be with us always.

Lord God, we ask your blessing
upon all leaders of nations and peoples.
We pray for your guidance
in the decisions they make this week
concerning the well-being of the world
and of the communities they serve.
We remember before you
all who strive for justice and peace in our world.
We ask for your protection upon all who are seekers or travellers.

Silence

Lord, guide our journeying:
be with us always.

Lord God, we give thanks
for all who have taught us
and guided us into the ways of truth,
those who shared with us their faith and their vision of life.
We ask your blessing upon all schools, colleges and universities.
We pray for our own homes and loved ones
and ask that our homes may show
your abiding presence and love.

Silence

Lord, guide our journeying:
be with us always.

Lord God, we ask your blessing
upon all who feel confused about life
and all who have lost their way.
We pray especially for all who are caught up
in the darkness of despair
and those involved in drugs or vice.
We pray for those who live a lie and cannot face the truth.
Lord, bless all who are suffering from broken relationships
and who are troubled in heart.
We remember all who are ill and fearful for their future.

Silence

Lord, guide our journeying:
be with us always.

Lord God, in your Son you have prepared for us
a place in your kingdom.
Lead us into the fullness of life and joy in your presence.
Bless all our loved ones departed,
that they may rejoice with your saints in glory.

Silence

Merciful Father,
accept these prayers
for the sake of your Son,
our Saviour Jesus Christ.
Amen.

4 Lord, walk with us

Blessed are you, Lord God,
for you are with us in our journeying and in our resting.
You are to be found in our homes and our daily lives.
You, Lord, are our hope and our strength:
in you we trust.
Blessed are you, Father, Son and Holy Spirit.

Lord, make yourself known to us
in church and through the Scriptures.
May we know you in the breaking of the bread,
in the break of day
and when our hearts are breaking.
Help us to see that you travel with us on the road of life
and you never leave us.
Fill us with your Spirit,
that we may proclaim the Good News
and tell others of your love.
We remember today all who are suffering because of their faith,
those who live in fear and those whose lives are restricted.

Silence

Lord, walk with us:
stay with us and help us.

We remember before you all travellers
and those who provide transport.
We ask your blessing
upon those who feel they are going into the dark
and to the end of life.
We pray for political prisoners
and the work of Amnesty International.
We remember all who are captive to doubt, fear or sin.

Silence

Lord, walk with us:
stay with us and help us.

Lord, may we be at home with you in our homes.
When our hearts burn within us,
may we know that you are near.
Help us to know you are with us
in all our dealings with others.
We remember today all who are lonely or feel rejected
and all who feel they are missing out on life.

Silence

Lord, walk with us:
stay with us and help us.

We pray for all who have lost vision and hope,
for all who are struggling with life.
We remember the broken-hearted,
those suffering from broken relationships,
all who are broken by illness or trouble,
all who can no longer cope on their own.
Lord, may they know you in their breaking
for you alone can make us whole.

Silence

Lord, walk with us:
stay with us and help us.

Lord, as in you we are born anew,
we remember before you the faithful departed.
We rejoice in the fellowship of all your saints.
May we share with them
and all our loved ones, both here and departed,
in the joy and fullness of life eternal.

Silence

Merciful Father,
accept these prayers
for the sake of your Son,
our Saviour Jesus Christ.
Amen.

5 The Lord is our Shepherd

Blessed are you, Lord our God,
for in your Son Jesus Christ
you have triumphed over darkness and death
and opened to us the way to eternal life.
Through Christ our Saviour
you have given us new hope and joy.
As we rejoice in his presence
may we give glory to you.
Blessed are you, Father, Son and Holy Spirit.

We give thanks for Jesus the Good Shepherd
and we pray for all who are called
to share in his ministry as shepherds
and guides of your flock.
We pray for all church leaders,
for preachers of the word
and ministers of the sacraments.
We ask your blessing upon all who are involved in pastoral care
and those who seek out the lost and the straying.

Silence

Hear us and help us,
through Jesus our Shepherd.

Loving God, we pray for all who express your love
in the way they care for others.
We pray for all who are striving for justice
and the relief of poverty.
We remember all social workers, carers and good neighbours.
We ask your blessing
upon all who feel at the mercy of circumstance
and who are unable to manage on their own.

Silence

Hear us and help us,
through Jesus our Shepherd.

Lord, bless our homes and our loved ones.
May we show respect and care for the world around us
and not be caught up with selfishness and greed.
Help us through our love for each other
to reveal your love in the world.

Silence

Hear us and help us,
through Jesus our Shepherd.

We give thanks that through Jesus
we can walk with confidence and hope.
We ask your blessing upon all who struggle
in darkness and fear,
all who feel lost
and those who are captives to vice and sin.
We remember friends and loved ones who are ill
and all the struggling people of our world.

Silence

Hear us and help us,
through Jesus our Shepherd.

We rejoice in the risen Lord and the promise of eternal life.
Lord, bless our loved ones departed.
May they share with your saints in glory.
To you and your unfailing love
we commit ourselves and the whole world
in time and for eternity.

Silence

Merciful Father,
accept these prayers
for the sake of your Son,
our Saviour Jesus Christ.
Amen.

6 God our helper

Blessed are you, Lord our God,
for you created this world
out of your goodness
and pour your love upon it.
All things are precious in your sight
and all are valued.
Blessed are you, Father, Son and Holy Spirit.

God, our Protection and strength,
we bring before you
all who are suffering for their faith,
all who are mocked, scorned, rejected
and in danger.
We remember those imprisoned
and those who suffer physical harm.
We pray for all who seek to proclaim your love
and to help in the healing of nations.
We ask your blessing
upon the Church to which we belong
and pray that we may use aright
the resources you have given us.

Silence

God, in your love and mercy,
hear us and help us.

God our Creator,
we ask you to bless and guide
all who work for the conservation of the earth
and for the care of each creature.
We pray for those involved in the protection
of endangered species
and we pray for those who seek to preserve
the rainforests and their inhabitants.

Silence

God, in your love and mercy,
hear us and help us.

We give thanks for the comfort and security
of our homes.
May we always be aware of the needs of others
and the danger of seeking the cheapest goods.
We ask your blessing upon our families and friends,
that they may know of your love and care.

Silence

God, in your love and mercy,
hear us and help us.

Loving God, we remember in your presence
all whose lives are endangered at this time.
We pray for those who have been involved in accidents
or acts of violence.
We remember those who have been driven off their land
or out of their homes.
We pray for all who are suffering in any way.

Silence

God, in your love and mercy,
hear us and help us.

Lord, you care for us in life and in death
and you offer us life eternal.
We ask you to give joy and peace
to our loved ones departed
and to all your saints.
May we come one day with them
to share in the fullness of your glory.

Silence

Merciful Father,
accept these prayers
for the sake of your Son,
our Saviour Jesus Christ.
Amen.

7 Loving God

Blessed are you, Lord our God,
for you have called us to be your people,
to represent you and to show your love.
By the power of your Spirit
enable us to live and work to your praise and glory.
Blessed are you, Father, Son and Holy Spirit.

We give thanks for all who have gone out in mission
and proclaimed the Good News in word and deed.
We remember especially
those who brought the Gospel to our land.
We ask your blessing upon preachers of the word
and on all who witness to you
by their lifestyle and example.
We pray for all who have never heard the Gospel
and those who are afraid to commit themselves.
We ask you to protect all missionaries who face hostility.

Silence

Loving God,
hear us and help us.

We remember all who live in a hostile environment,
those who are suffering from war or oppression.
We ask your blessing
upon all who seek to bring peace and healing
to the divisions of our world
and all who strive to bring freedom and justice
to nations and individuals.
We remember the work of the United Nations
and Amnesty International.

Silence

Loving God,
hear us and help us.

Father, we thank you for the love of our homes
and ask your blessing upon our families and friends.
We remember all who suffer
from rejection or violence in their homes.
We pray for all who have been taken into care
or those living on the streets of our cities and towns.

Silence

Loving God,
hear us and help us.

Father, we give thanks for your healing love.
We remember before you all suffering people,
the ill and the hungry,
the world's poor and the unemployed.
We ask your blessing upon all who are terminally ill
and those who are caring for them.
We pray for helpers who feel exhausted
or who feel they are not appreciated.

Silence

Loving God,
hear us and help us.

We give thanks that, through Christ,
the way to the fullness of your kingdom
is open to us.
We pray for our loved ones departed.
We commend them to you
as we do the world and ourselves.

Silence

Merciful Father,
accept these prayers
for the sake of your Son,
our Saviour Jesus Christ.
Amen.

8 Renewal and peace

Blessed are you, Lord our God,
for you are a very present help in trouble.
You are more ready to hear than we to pray,
and willing to give us more than we desire or deserve.
We come to you for rest, for renewal,
for the strength to do what you would have us do.
Blessed are you, Father, Son and Holy Spirit.

We give thanks for the Church throughout the world.
We remember today all who are weary in their service
and all who are in danger of losing faith.
We pray for priests and pastors
who are working in difficult areas and with little support.
We ask your blessing
upon all who are seeking to share the burdens
of those with great responsibilities.
We pray for all who are carers
and who are giving support to others.

Silence

Lord, we come to you:
renew us and give us peace.

As we rejoice in the gift of life,
we remember the world-weary,
the overwrought and the anxious.
We pray for all who are laden with troubles or guilt.
We ask your blessing upon all who are overworked or oppressed
and those who are fearful for the future.
We remember those who have lost the joy of living
and all who cannot easily relax.

Silence

Lord, we come to you:
renew us and give us peace.

We give thanks for our friends and loved ones,
for those who share our joys and our sorrows.
We remember all who have been a support
and comfort to us.
We pray for families where there is tension and stress
and we remember all who feel lonely and without help.

Silence

Lord, we come to you:
renew us and give us peace.

We give thanks, O Lord, for continual support
and we pray for all who feel uncared for or unwanted.
We remember all who are at the point of breaking
and all those who have broken down.
We ask your blessing upon all who are ill
and are finding life difficult.
We pray for all who seek to be a help and a support.

Silence

Lord, we come to you:
renew us and give us peace.

We ask your blessing
upon all who have found their rest in you.
We remember our friends and loved ones departed.
May they find in you rest, renewal
and the joy of the resurrection.

Silence

Merciful Father,
accept these prayers
for the sake of your Son,
our Saviour Jesus Christ.
Amen.

9 God's provision

Blessed are you, Lord our God,
for you provide food for our daily needs
and for all creatures.
You give food, resources and talents
for us to share with others and give you glory.
Blessed are you, Father, Son and Holy Spirit.

We ask your blessing
upon all who hunger and thirst
for righteousness and the coming of your kingdom.
We remember all who feel their lives are parched and dry
and who suffer from spiritual hunger.
May the Good News be brought to all
who feel empty and that life is meaningless.
We bring before you all who go out in mission
and all who seek to proclaim your love.

Silence

Renewing and refreshing God,
hear us and help us.

We ask your blessing
upon all who lack the necessary resources for well-being.
We pray for all who are suffering
from hunger and poverty,
all who struggle due to injustice and greed.
We remember all who have lost crops and livestock
through famine, drought or war.
We pray for the work of Christian Aid
and for all who seek to bring relief
to the hungry and poor.

Silence

Renewing and refreshing God,
hear us and help us.

We give thanks for our loved ones,
for all who have cared and provided for us.
We ask your blessing upon all who work
to give us what we need.
We pray for all farmers and food providers,
for shop workers
and all who bring our food to the markets.
We ask your blessing upon our families
and our neighbours.

Silence

Renewing and refreshing God,
hear us and help us.

We remember all who feel weary with life,
drained of energy and no longer able to cope.
We pray for all who struggle against great odds.
We ask your blessing upon all who feel alone
and that no one cares for them.
We pray for all who are ill at home or in hospital.

Silence

Renewing and refreshing God,
hear us and help us.

We give thanks that you give life and life eternal,
that you are a renewing and restoring God.
As we rejoice in the resurrection,
we ask your blessing upon our loved ones departed.
May they know the peace and glory of your kingdom.

Silence

Merciful Father,
accept these prayers
for the sake of your Son,
our Saviour Jesus Christ.
Amen.

10 The storms of life

Blessed are you, Lord our God,
for you are a very present help in trouble.
You are ready to hear our cry
and come to our aid.
Lord, help us not to be afraid
but to put our trust and hope in you.
May we ever rejoice in your love and care.
Blessed are you, Father, Son and Holy Spirit,
one God for ever.

Lord, you have created us out of love
and for your love.
We ask for your protection
in the troubles and storms of life.
Bless all Christians who are struggling against great odds.
We pray for those who are suffering
from persecution, violence or ridicule.
We remember those whose lives are at risk
and those who are exhausted.

Silence

Lord, in the storms of life,
hear us and help us.

We give thanks for the work of the Mission to Seafarers
and those who go out in lifeboats.
We pray for all whose work is upon the sea.
We ask your blessing upon fishermen,
merchant seamen and the Royal Navy.
We remember today all who are caught up
in storms, in earthquakes, floods or droughts.

Silence

Lord, in the storms of life,
hear us and help us.

We give you thanks
for the safety and protection of our homes.
We pray for all who are struggling
with problems of debt
or whose relationships are breaking down.
We pray for the work of Shelter
and remember all who are homeless
and living on the streets of our towns and cities.

Silence

Lord, in the storms of life,
hear us and help us.

Lord, we pray for your blessing
upon the world-weary, the worried and worn,
all who feel overwhelmed and unable to cope.
We remember all who are ill at home or in hospital
and those who care for them.
We pray especially for any involved in accidents
or whose illness finds no cure.

Silence

Lord, in the storms of life,
hear us and help us.

Lord, stand by us when the last great storm
seeks to overwhelm us
and we feel we are sinking beneath the waves.
Help us to know that in you we will not perish
but have everlasting life.
To you we commit all our loved ones departed:
may they rejoice in your presence and in your peace.

Silence

Merciful Father,
accept these prayers
for the sake of your Son,
our Saviour Jesus Christ.
Amen.

11 Save us and help us

Blessed are you, Lord our God,
for in your love you sent your Son Jesus Christ
to be our Saviour.
You deliver us from the darkness of sin and death
and open to us the way to eternal life.
Blessed are you, Father, Son and Holy Spirit.
To you be praise and glory for ever.

We give thanks for all who have witnessed
to your love and saving power.
We ask your blessing upon all preachers of the word
and ministers of the sacraments,
that they may keep us aware of your presence
and wonderful power.
We pray for all who are growing in the faith,
and remember before you
all who attend study groups and Bible class.
We pray especially today
for all who are struggling with their faith
and those who have fallen away.

Silence

Jesus, Saviour of the world,
we look to you to save and help us.

We give thanks for the wonders of creation
and the mystery of life.
We ask your blessing upon all who suffer
from injustice, war or violence.
We remember those caught up in natural disasters
and struggle due to famine or flood.
We pray for those
who feel life has no purpose or meaning
and all who are tempted to despair.

Silence

Jesus, Saviour of the world,
we look to you to save and help us.

We give thanks for the love of our homes and dear ones,
for all the help and encouragement they have given us.
We ask your blessing on homes where life is restricted
and where there is little joy.
We remember all who are homeless, all who are deeply in debt
and all who are uncertain of their future.

Silence

Jesus, Saviour of the world,
we look to you to save and help us.

We give thanks for all who share in your healing
and bringing of peace to peoples and nations.
We ask your blessing upon all who are struggling
against evil or with illness.
We remember especially
those for whom life brings little joy or hope.
We pray for friends and loved ones who are ill
and all who feel lonely or frightened at this time.

Silence

Jesus, Saviour of the world,
we look to you to save and help us.

We give thanks that through Christ
we are offered eternal life.
We ask your blessing upon all your saints
and our loved ones departed.
We commend them, this world and ourselves
to your unfailing love.

Silence

Merciful Father,
accept these prayers
for the sake of your Son,
our Saviour Jesus Christ.
Amen.

12 Heal our infirmities

Blessed are you, Lord our God,
for you have revealed your love and forgiveness
through your Son Jesus Christ.
Through him we are ransomed, healed and forgiven.
As we have freely received,
may we freely give.
Blessed are you, Father, Son and Holy Spirit.

God of mercy, we come to you for forgiveness and renewal.
We ask you to bless all who are seeking to change their lives
and live to serve others and to glorify you.
Though we are unworthy
we seek your acceptance of us.
May your Church reveal your love
in its care for all who come to it.
We pray today for prison chaplains and clergy
who work in areas of crime and vice.

Silence

Lord, forgive our sins
and heal our infirmities.

God of mercy, we ask your blessing
upon the poor, hungry and homeless of the world,
and all migrant and displaced peoples.
We remember nations that are in great debt
and the work of the world banks and governments
to relieve this debt.
We pray for all who are bankrupt
and all who have lost the little that they had.
We bring before you all who are fearful for their future.

Silence

Lord, forgive our sins
and heal our infirmities.

God of mercy, you have given to us richly;
may we richly give.
Let us not hoard or squander
the good things you have given us.
Let us help those in need and use our gifts to your glory.
We ask your blessing upon our homes
and upon all who have enriched our lives
by their goodness and love.

Silence

Lord, forgive our sins
and heal our infirmities.

God of mercy, we pray
for all who have become hard-hearted,
all who are unable to forgive and all who seek revenge.
Through your love may they find a change of attitude and heart.
We ask your blessing upon all who are abused,
all who are used as cheap labour
and all who do not receive a fair wage.
We bring before you friends and loved ones who are ill.

Silence

Lord, forgive our sins
and heal our infirmities.

God of mercy, we give thanks
for all who have witnessed to your love and generosity.
We rejoice in the fellowship of the saints.
We commend our loved ones departed,
this world and ourselves
to your unfailing love and mercy.

Silence

Merciful Father,
accept these prayers
for the sake of your Son,
our Saviour Jesus Christ.
Amen.

13 Forgiving God

Blessed are you, Lord our God,
for you accept us in our sin,
you forgive all who are penitent
and give us the opportunity of newness of life.
Blessed are you, Father, Son and Holy Spirit.

Loving and forgiving God,
we rejoice in your presence
and we remember before you
all who seek to build up your Church in love.
We ask your blessing upon all who are being prepared
for baptism or confirmation.
We pray for all who seek forgiveness
and want to start afresh.

Silence

Forgiving God,
hear us and help us.

Loving and forgiving God,
we remember in your presence
all who work for reconciliation
between peoples and nations.
We pray for all who seek to heal old hurts
and historical grievances.
Bless all peacemakers
and all who work to bring unity and understanding
within communities.
We pray for the work of the United Nations
and all who seek to bring justice and fair dealings
to our world.

Silence

Forgiving God,
hear us and help us.

Loving and forgiving God,
may our homes reflect your love.
Forgive our petty divisions and jealousies,
our quarrelling and our anger.
Lord, through our homes and loved ones
teach us forgiveness, tolerance and compassion.
May our homes and our community
be seen as caring and loving.

Silence

Forgiving God,
hear us and help us.

Loving and forgiving God,
we remember in your presence
all whose lives are spoiled by hatred
and the desire for revenge.
We pray for all who feel they cannot be forgiven
and who cannot forgive.
We ask your blessing
upon all who are troubled in mind or spirit
and all who are tempted to give up hope.

Silence

Forgiving God,
hear us and help us.

Loving and forgiving God, we give thanks
that we are ransomed, healed, forgiven.
We ask your blessing
upon our friends and loved ones departed,
that knowing your forgiveness
they may rejoice in your love.

Silence

Merciful Father,
accept these prayers
for the sake of your Son,
our Saviour Jesus Christ.
Amen.

14 God's strength and guidance

Blessed are you, God our Father,
for you have sent your Son to be our Saviour.
In him you have delivered us
from the dominion of darkness
and made us children of the day and of light.
Blessed are you, Father, Son and Holy Spirit.

Loving Father, we give you thanks
for the coming of our Lord Jesus Christ
for in him you have opened the gate to eternal life.
Bless all who seek to proclaim the Good News,
all who preach the word and go out in mission.
We remember all who witness in their daily life
and all who seek to serve you faithfully.

Silence

Holy God, holy and strong One,
hear us and help us.

Loving Father, we ask your blessing
upon all who have important decisions to make this week.
We pray for those who are rulers and politicians,
for scientists and research workers,
for judges and all who strive to bring peace.
We remember all who find it hard to remain faithful and loyal
and pray that they may be given new strength and courage.

Silence

Holy God, holy and strong One,
hear us and help us.

Loving Father, we give thanks
for our homes and our loved ones.
We pray for all who have influenced our lives
through their example and teaching.

We remember all families
where relationships are breaking down
or life has become hard.
We ask your blessing
upon those who have to make difficult decisions
about their homes, their relationships or their way of life.

Silence

Holy God, holy and strong One,
hear us and help us.

Loving Father, we remember all
who are confused by the many choices in life
and who find it hard to cope.
We pray for those who have lost their freedom
and all who suffer from tyranny.
We ask your blessing upon all who are ill
and those who have decided they need to go into care.

Silence

Holy God, holy and strong One,
hear us and help us.

Loving Father, we thank you
that Jesus came down to lift us up
into the fullness of your kingdom.
We rejoice in the fellowship of your saints in glory.
We remember before you
all our friends and loved ones departed.
We commit our lives and all of your creation
to your unfailing love.

Silence

Merciful Father,
accept these prayers
for the sake of your Son,
our Saviour Jesus Christ.
Amen.

15 Saviour of all

Blessed are you, Lord our God,
for you are our Creator
and you have called us to know you
and proclaim your love.
Help us to be aware that you speak to us through the Scriptures
and through those who tell of your presence and power today.
Blessed are you, Father, Son and Holy Spirit.

Father Creator, raise up among us
prophets and preachers
who will tell of your mighty acts and your saving power.
To scientists and research workers
give vision of the wonder and mystery of your world.
Bless your Church with an awareness of
and living relationship with Christ,
that it may witness to the power of the resurrection.
We pray for all Christians who are suffering
from persecution or rejection.

Silence

Lord and Saviour of all,
hear us and help us.

Father Creator, we ask your blessing
upon leaders of peoples
and all who influence our lives by their decisions.
Give them wisdom and respect in all their dealings.
We pray for all who work in the field of genetics
and those who influence our world by their actions.
We remember all who seek to show us
how to care for the world.

Silence

Lord and Saviour of all,
hear us and help us.

Father Creator, we give thanks
for our homes and our loved ones.
We ask your blessing upon all homes
where there is tension and misunderstanding.
We pray for marriages that are struggling
and families that are in danger of falling apart.
We remember all who feel rejected or neglected.

Silence

Lord and Saviour of all,
hear us and help us.

Father Creator, we give thanks
for all you have given to us.
We pray for the world's poor, the oppressed
and all who are suffering from violence.
We remember those who have been driven off their own land
and all who are refugees.
We ask your blessing upon all who are ill
or who have been injured
and all who are fearful for their future.

Silence

Lord and Saviour of all,
hear us and help us.

Father Creator, we give thanks
for Jesus Christ the living Lord
and for the power of his resurrection.
We commit to your keeping our loved ones departed,
that they may rejoice in the fullness of your kingdom,
and we pray that we may share with them
in the knowledge of your love.

Silence

Merciful Father,
accept these prayers
for the sake of your Son,
our Saviour Jesus Christ.
Amen.

16 Raise us up

Blessed are you, Lord our God,
for out of your love
you call us to know and to love you.
Lord, may we come to know you,
and in knowing you, love you,
and in loving you, serve you,
whose service is perfect freedom.
Blessed are you, Father, Son and Holy Spirit.

Lord, as you have called us
make us worthy of our calling.
We ask your blessing
upon all who seek to fulfil their calling in life.
We pray for those who are called to proclaim the Gospel
and to give account of you.
We pray for preachers and evangelists.
We ask your guidance
upon all who are called to witness to you,
to your power and your love.

Silence

We come to your love:
heal us and raise us up.

We remember before you all who suffer from rejection and scorn.
We pray for homeless people, for refugees and the world's poor.
We ask your blessing upon all who are used as cheap labour
or who are abused by taskmasters.
We pray for all who suffer from injustice
or the lack of fair trade.

Silence

We come to your love:
heal us and raise us up.

We give thanks for our homes and our loved ones.
As we ask your blessing upon them,
we remember homes where there is sorrow and suffering.
We pray for those who are struggling
due to the illness of a loved one,
those who have got deeply into debt
and those who feel drained and exhausted.

Silence

We come to your love:
heal us and raise us up.

We give thanks
for all who work in the healing professions,
and we pray for our own doctors and health workers.
We remember all who are denied healing and help
through poverty or war.
We ask your blessing upon all who are caring
for a loved one who is terminally ill,
and for the work of hospices.

Silence

We come to your love:
heal us and raise us up.

We give thanks for all you have lifted from death
into the fullness of life eternal.
We rejoice with all the faithful departed
who are where sorrow and pain are no more.
To you, to your power and love,
we commit this world,
our loved ones and ourselves
now and for ever.

Silence

Merciful Father,
accept these prayers
for the sake of your Son,
our Saviour Jesus Christ.
Amen.

17 Help in trouble

Blessed are you, Lord our God,
for amidst the trials and troubles of the world
you are present and ready to help us.
You sent your Son
so that we should not perish
but have eternal life.
Blessed are you, Father, Son and Holy Spirit.

We give thanks to you, O Lord,
for the Church
and the hope that it brings to troubled lives.
We ask your blessing upon Christians
who are being persecuted for their faith
or who risk their lives in the care of others.
We remember all relief agencies
and those who work in war-torn areas,
in areas of earthquake or famine.

Silence

Lord, we put our trust in you:
hear us and help us.

We give thanks, O Lord,
for all who seek to bring peace and harmony to our world.
We ask your blessing upon leaders of nations
and all peacekeeping forces.
We pray especially
for those whose lives are endangered at this time.

Silence

Lord, we put our trust in you:
hear us and help us.

We give thanks, O Lord,
for our homes and our loved ones.
We ask your blessing
upon all who have been driven out of their homes
through acts of violence, natural disaster or debt.
We pray for those who find they can no longer cope
in their own home.

Silence

Lord, we put our trust in you:
hear us and help us.

We give thanks, O Lord,
for the healing services.
We pray for all doctors and nurses,
for paramedics and those who work in ambulances
or rescue vehicles.
We ask your blessing upon all whose world has fallen apart
through sickness or loss of a loved one.

Silence

Lord, we put our trust in you:
hear us and help us.

We give thanks, O Lord,
for the gift of eternal life.
We rejoice in the fellowship of all your saints
and ask your blessing upon our loved ones departed.
May we all share with you in the fullness of your kingdom.

Silence

Merciful Father,
accept these prayers
for the sake of your Son,
our Saviour Jesus Christ.
Amen.

18 God our Redeemer

Blessed are you, Lord our God,
for you are always ready to help and protect us.
You are a present help in all our needs and troubles.
Blessed are you, Father, Son and Holy Spirit.

God our Redeemer, we thank you
for the Church throughout the whole world.
We remember especially today
the Coptic Church of Egypt.
We ask your blessing upon all Christians
who are being persecuted or penalised for their faith.
We pray for Christians who are exiled
or imprisoned for their beliefs.
We remember all who are struggling with doubt
and those who lack any teaching in the faith.

Silence

God our Redeemer,
hear us and help us.

We give thanks for our land and its freedom.
We remember in your presence
all who are refugees or homeless at this time.
We ask your blessing upon the world's poor
and all who are unable to use their abilities and talents.
Bless the work of Fair Trade organisations
and all who strive to relieve injustice and poverty.

Silence

God our Redeemer,
hear us and help us.

We give thanks for the love and protection of our parents.
We ask your blessing upon our homes
and all our loved ones,
that they may live in peace and be free from poverty.
We remember all children who have been taken into care
and all families who find it difficult to cope.
We pray for any parents who have lost a child
over this last year.

Silence

God our Redeemer,
hear us and help us.

We give thanks for the medical profession
and for all who care for our well-being.
We ask your blessing upon all who are ill
at home or in hospital.
We remember any who have been injured
in accidents or through acts of violence.
We pray especially for families
where there is a child who is ill or suffering.

Silence

God our Redeemer,
hear us and help us.

We give thanks that you are our Redeemer;
that you seek that we should not perish
but have everlasting life.
We remember friends and loved ones
who are departed from us.
We rejoice in the fellowship of all your saints
and ask that we may share with them in your glory.

Silence

Merciful Father,
accept these prayers
for the sake of your Son,
our Saviour Jesus Christ.
Amen.

19 Deliver us from evil

Blessed are you, Lord our God,
for you give us grace to defeat evil
and to resist temptation.
In our troubles you are our strength and our support.
You bring us to eternal life.
Blessed are you, Father, Son and Holy Spirit,
for ever and ever.

Lord, bless your people who are struggling with temptation.
Guide your Church, that it may lead others to do your will
and to live in love and peace with all.
Lord, help us to make others aware
of the deep spiritual things within our world:
that we are all called to work with you.
Help us to do your will
and so live in your kingdom.

Silence

Lord, hear us
and deliver us from evil.

We remember before you
all who are suffering through sin, violence and war.
We pray for peoples and nations
that are divided against each other
through ancient wrongs and through greed.
We pray for all who are sorely tempted to do wrong.
Lord, show us all the peace we should give
and the peace we should forgo.

Silence

Lord, hear us
and deliver us from evil.

We ask your blessing upon our homes and families.
We bring before you all who are suffering
from broken relationships and broken homes.
We pray for those who have been rejected
by their families
and all who feel they have been betrayed in love.
Bless all who work to bring reconciliation
and new hope to separated peoples.

Silence

Lord, hear us
and deliver us from evil.

We give thanks for all who share in healing
and the restoring of well-being to all who suffer.
We remember all who are in pain
or distress at this time.
We ask your blessing
upon all who are separated from loved ones
through illness or disability
and all who can no longer cope on their own.

Silence

Lord, hear us
and deliver us from evil.

We give thanks for the forgiveness of sins
and the hope of eternal life.
We rejoice in the fellowship
of all the saints and the faithful
who are now in your kingdom.
We pray for our loved ones departed.
May we all at the last share in the glory
of your kingdom and your love.

Silence

Merciful Father,
accept these prayers
for the sake of your Son,
our Saviour Jesus Christ.
Amen.

20 Scatter the darkness

Blessed are you, Lord God,
Giver of life and Creator of love.
We give you thanks and praise
for the light of each day
and for the light of the Gospel
as revealed in our Saviour Jesus Christ.
We rejoice in the life that you give us
and we delight in your presence.
Blessed are you, Father, Son and Holy Spirit.

As we give thanks for the light of Jesus Christ
we ask that this light may shine in our lives
and in the whole Church.
We ask your blessing on all who proclaim the Gospel
and who teach the word.
We pray for all who are seeking
to revive and promote faith in you and your love.
May the Church grow in love,
in witness and in number.

Silence

Lord God of light,
scatter the darkness from our world.

We ask your blessing upon rulers and leaders
who have difficult decisions to make concerning the world
and who are often not sure which way to go.
We pray for all who work
to bring freedom and justice to all people,
those who seek to relieve the poor
and care for the oppressed.
We pray for those who feel
that they are working in the dark
and unable to find their way.

Silence

Lord God of light,
scatter the darkness from our world.

Lord, we ask that all darkness be dispersed
from our hearts and our communities.
May we help to bring your light and life
to our homes and to all our relationships.
We ask your blessing upon our families and friends
and upon all with whom we work or play.

Silence

Lord God of light,
scatter the darkness from our world.

We remember today all who walk in darkness
and in the shadow of fear or death.
We ask your blessing upon the fearful,
the anxious and the troubled.
We pray for all who are in the darkness
of doubt or despair.
We bring before you friends and loved ones who are ill
or who are finding it hard to cope with life.

Silence

Lord God of light,
scatter the darkness from our world.

We give thanks for the fullness of eternal life.
We ask your blessing upon our loved ones
who have entered into the fullness of your kingdom
and all the faithful departed.
We pray for the day when we may all see you more clearly
and walk without fear in your light.

Silence

Merciful Father,
accept these prayers
for the sake of your Son,
our Saviour Jesus Christ.
Amen.

21 Life and love (1)

Blessed are you, Lord our God,
for you have created us in your own image:
you have called us to reflect
your love and your forgiveness to all.
You give us power to share in your grace.
Blessed are you, Father, Son and Holy Spirit.

Lord, as you reveal your love to us,
help us to show that love
towards all whom we meet.
We ask your blessing
upon all who seek to reveal your grace
and to walk in the way of your laws.
We remember before you
all who preach and teach of your love.
We ask your blessing
upon all who study the Scriptures
in groups or in schools.

Silence

Lord of life and love,
hear us and help us.

Lord, as you teach us to respect each other,
help us to respect the earth and all its creatures.
Give us a reverence towards all of your creation.
Guide all who care for the resources of our planet
and the environment in which we live.
We pray for areas that have been devastated
by war or greed.

Silence

Lord of life and love,
hear us and help us.

Lord, forgive our times of anger and hatred
and help us to live at peace with each other.
May our communities be places
where no one is belittled and no one oppressed.
We pray for our homes and our loved ones.

Silence

Lord of life and love,
hear us and help us.

Lord, we remember before you
all who are suffering through violence or abuse.
We pray especially for those
whose lives are marred by their past or present sins.
We remember also today all who are struggling
with pain or chronic illness
and all who can no longer cope with life on their own.

Silence

Lord of life and love,
hear us and help us.

We rejoice that nothing can separate us
from the love of God in Christ Jesus.
We ask your blessing
upon our friends and loved ones departed.
As we rejoice in the fellowship of all your saints,
we commend this world, all peoples and ourselves
to your unfailing love.

Silence

Merciful Father,
accept these prayers
for the sake of your Son,
our Saviour Jesus Christ.
Amen.

22 Life and love (2)

Blessed are you, Lord our God,
for you have created us all out of love
and for your love.
Even when in our sin and foolishness
we go against you and leave you,
you are there and seek us out in love.
Blessed are you, Father, Son and Holy Spirit.

Loving God, may your Church throughout the world
show your love for all peoples and nations.
Bless all who seek to heal divisions
and to do away with prejudice.
Give courage to all who reach out to those in need
and who seek to welcome the rejected.
May your Church reflect your saving love.

Silence

Lord of life and love,
hear us and help us.

Loving God, we ask forgiveness
for the sin and arrogance that divides us
and creates barriers between nations and peoples.
We pray with love for all minority groups,
for those who are judged by their race,
colour or history.
We remember all who are refugees, homeless
or outcasts of society.
We ask your blessing upon all who work
to bring a new unity and understanding
between divided peoples.

Silence

Lord of life and love,
hear us and help us.

Loving God, we thank you for our homes
and for all who have accepted us
in love and generosity.
We ask your blessing upon our homes
and the community in which we live.
We pray for all who are suffering from broken relationships
and all who feel estranged from the world around them.

Silence

Lord of life and love,
hear us and help us.

Loving God, we give thanks for our health and well-being.
We ask your blessing upon all who are ill
at home or in hospital.
We remember today all who suffer
from autism or schizophrenia
and all who are mentally ill.
We ask your blessing upon all
who are separated from their loved ones through illness
and all who feel rejected.

Silence

Lord of life and love,
hear us and help us.

Loving God, in your redeeming love
you accept us and welcome us.
We ask you to give joy and peace
to all our loved ones who have departed this life:
may they know the fullness of salvation.
To you and your love we commit the whole world,
our loved ones and ourselves.

Silence

Merciful Father,
accept these prayers
for the sake of your Son,
our Saviour Jesus Christ.
Amen.

23 Health and salvation

Blessed are you, Lord our God,
for you have called us to know you
and to abide with you.
You have called us to love you and to tell of you.
Blessed are you, Father, Son and Holy Spirit,
for you have called us into life and life eternal.
Blessed be God for ever.

Father, we ask your blessing upon the Church,
that it may grow in love for you,
that it may grow in holiness,
that it may grow in size.
We remember before you
all who reach out in mission
to tell of your love and your saving power.
We pray for preachers of the word
and teachers of the faith,
and we ask that we may all share
in bringing others to you.

Silence

Lord, we pray to you:
you are our health and salvation.

Lord God,
we pray for all who are being exploited by others.
We remember the poor and the homeless
and we ask your blessing
upon all who care for refugees and deprived peoples.
We pray for all who lack any moral or spiritual guidance
and who are being led astray by people around them.

Silence

Lord, we pray to you:
you are our health and salvation.

We give thanks for those who taught us the faith
and who set us an example by their lives.
We ask your blessing upon our home,
our loved ones and all who have cared for us.
We pray for all who suffer from neglect, violence
or a lack of love.

Silence

Lord, we pray to you:
you are our health and salvation.

God, in you is our peace and our hope.
We remember in your presence
all who are ill or suffering.
We pray especially for any who feel confused by life
and who are not able to cope.
We pray for all who are caught up in drug abuse or vice.

Silence

Lord, we pray to you:
you are our health and salvation.

We give thanks for your redeeming love
and for the gift of life eternal.
We pray for all our loved ones departed
and commend them, this world and ourselves
to your unfailing love.

Silence

Merciful Father,
accept these prayers
for the sake of your Son,
our Saviour Jesus Christ.
Amen.

24 Lighten our darkness

Blessed are you, Lord our God,
for you have called us out of darkness
to be children of light.
The bright light of your presence
scatters the darkness within us
and is a guide on our journey.
Blessed are you, Father, Son and Holy Spirit.

We rejoice that in Christ we know
that light is stronger than darkness
and life is stronger than death.
Give your Church the courage
to proclaim the Good News to all people.
We remember all who are in doubt
or who are struggling with their faith.
We pray for those who have lost faith
and walk in darkness.

Silence

Lord, hear us:
come, lighten our darkness.

Lord of all, we bring before you
the troubles and dangers of peoples and nations,
the war-torn and the world-weary.
We ask your blessing
upon communities seeking to rebuild their lives
in peace and hope.
We pray for all rulers, governments
and leaders of people,
that they will strive for justice and peace.

Silence

Lord, hear us:
come, lighten our darkness.

Bless our homes with the light of your presence.
We pray for our loved ones and friends,
for our neighbours and our community.
May the bright light of Christ shine within us
and scatter any darkness that is around us.

Silence

Lord, hear us:
come, lighten our darkness.

We remember all who are struggling
with illness or with fear.
We ask your blessing
upon all who are in hospital,
all who have been injured
through violence or accidents.
We pray for all who are fearful of the future.
We pray also for the bereaved and the lonely.

Silence

Lord, hear us:
come, lighten our darkness.

We remember all who are nearing death
and those who care for them.
May they trust in you and in eternal life.
We commend all our loved ones departed
to your love and your kingdom.

Silence

Merciful Father,
accept these prayers
for the sake of your Son,
our Saviour Jesus Christ.
Amen.

25 Rise and shine

Blessed are you, Lord our God,
for you come to us and abide with us always.
Your light scatters the darkness from before us
and you invite us to let this shine through us
and reveal you to the world.
In your love help us to be children of light.
Blessed are you, Father, Son and Holy Spirit.

Lord of light and love,
we ask your blessing upon the Church
throughout the world.
We pray especially for areas
where the faith has grown dim
and vision has been lost.
We remember all who are struggling
against dark and evil forces.
We pray for all who seek
to bring the light of Christ to others.

Silence

Lord of light,
awaken us to your presence.

Lord of light and love,
strengthen all who are on their guard against evil
and seek to bring peace and harmony to our world.
We remember before you
all who are suffering
through oppression or violence,
all who are used as cheap labour
and all who are without proper homes or enough food.
Bless all who work tirelessly for their relief.

Silence

Lord of light,
awaken us to your presence.

Lord of light and love,
make us alert to your presence with us and in our homes.
Bless and protect our families and our friends.
Make us alert to the needs of our community,
where we can help and be of use.
Let us not miss opportunities of showing your love.

Silence

Lord of light,
awaken us to your presence.

Lord of light and love,
bless all whose lives are darkened by illness or tragedy.
We remember all who feel afraid
and those who regret work undone
or doing what they should not have done.
We pray for all who are terminally ill
and all who can no longer look after themselves.

Silence

Lord of light,
awaken us to your presence.

Lord of light and love,
we ask your blessing upon all our friends and loved ones
who are departed from us.
May they rejoice in your light and love
in your kingdom.
We pray for all your saints
and all who have reflected your light in the world.

Silence

Merciful Father,
accept these prayers
for the sake of your Son,
our Saviour Jesus Christ.
Amen.

26 God refresh us

Blessed are you, Lord our God.
You give us life
and you continually renew and refresh us
with your presence and your love.
You are the strength of the weak
and the light to all who walk in darkness.
Blessed are you, Father, Son and Holy Spirit.

Lord God, may we reveal your joy and power
in our daily living.
We ask your blessing upon the Church,
that it may be obedient to your word
and seek to bring others to know your glory.
We ask you to bless all preachers and teachers of the faith,
that they may have the power
to reveal you and your love to others.

Silence

God of love and joy,
hear us and refresh us.

Lord, our Creator,
we pray that we may use the world aright.
Let us not squander or waste the resources you have given us
but use them to your glory and the benefit of all.
We pray for all who monitor our planet and its resources.
We ask your blessing upon scientists and politicians
and all who work to care for and improve our world.
We remember today
all who suffer from deprivation, from poverty,
from hunger or from homelessness.

Silence

God of love and joy,
hear us and refresh us.

We give thanks for our own home
and all you have given us.
We pray for those who provide us with our food
and our daily needs.
We ask your blessing upon all who work
to provide good homes and shelter
to the poor of our world.

Silence

God of love and joy,
hear us and refresh us.

We remember today all who are running out of resources.
We pray for the fearful and the anxious,
the sad and the lonely.
We ask your blessing upon all who are ill
and cannot cope on their own.
We remember all who, through ageing or illness,
need regular care and attention.
We pray for all carers
and all who work in the health service.

Silence

God of love and joy,
hear us and refresh us.

We rejoice in life and that you give us life eternal.
Renewing and restoring God,
we remember in your presence our loved ones departed
and ask that they may rejoice in your presence
and in the fullness of life eternal.
We commend them, the world and ourselves
to your unfailing love.

Silence

Merciful Father,
accept these prayers
for the sake of your Son,
our Saviour Jesus Christ.
Amen.

27 You have called us

Blessed are you, Lord our God,
for you have called us into life and to love you.
You have called us to proclaim your love and power
in all the world.
Lord, send us out in the power of your Spirit,
that we may tell of you and your abiding presence.
Blessed are you, Father, Son and Holy Spirit.

Lord, we ask your blessing upon your Church,
that we may show signs of being One in you,
holy and dedicated to being apostolic
as we reach out to all peoples.
We pray for all who are reaching out to others
in your name and in love.
Bless and guide all who preach the word
and all who share in your healing ministry.
We remember those involved in a pastoral ministry
and those who work to relieve the distress and sorrow
of people and nations.

Silence

Lord, as you have called us,
hear us and help us.

We pray for all who are called to govern
and all who influence the minds of others.
We pray for leaders of industry
and great multi-national companies
and for all they work with.
Lord, help us to show our care for the earth
and our respect for the individual in all that we do.
We remember those whose lives are blighted
by the greed or insensitivity of others.

Silence

Lord, as you have called us,
hear us and help us.

We give thanks because you show us your love
through those who love us.
We ask your blessing upon our homes and our loved ones.
We pray for homes where there is stress and distress.
We remember all who are finding it difficult to cope
and those who are deeply in debt.
We pray for all who are seeking to help those in need.

Silence

Lord, as you have called us,
hear us and help us.

We give thanks for all involved in the healing ministry.
We ask your blessing upon doctors and nurses
and all the emergency services.
We pray for those who are good neighbours and carers
in their local community.
We remember all who are frustrated
through illness or a disability,
and all who are struggling with life.

Silence

Lord, as you have called us,
hear us and help us.

We rejoice in the fellowship of all your saints,
in all who have heard your call and done your will.
We ask your blessing upon our loved ones
who are departed from us.
May we all share in the joy of your love and your kingdom.

Silence

Merciful Father,
accept these prayers
for the sake of your Son,
our Saviour Jesus Christ.
Amen.

28 Christian service

Blessed are you, Lord our God,
for you give us life,
you give us love,
you give us yourself.
Lord, may we learn to give our life, our love,
ourselves to you,
for it is in such giving
that we open our lives to you.
Blessed are you, Father, Son and Holy Spirit.

We give you thanks, O Lord,
for all who have heard your call
and served you faithfully.
We give thanks
for those who have shared their faith with us.
We ask your blessing upon all who seek to witness
to your abiding presence and your love.
We pray for all who are seeking to fulfil their calling in life.
We pray for schools, colleges and universities.
We remember especially today
all who are being prepared for baptism,
confirmation or ordination.

Silence

Lord, hear us
and help us to serve you.

We give thanks for all who provide us with our daily food.
We ask your blessing upon all who are involved
in growing or supplying our food.
We remember before you
all who are being used as cheap labour
and we pray for fair trade and justice.
May we all use the resources of the world
with care and respect.

Silence

Lord, hear us
and help us to serve you.

We give thanks for our homes and our loved ones,
for all who have enriched us
by their love and generosity.
We ask your blessing upon all who are struggling
through debt, poverty or homelessness.
We pray for all who feel used, abused or unloved.

Silence

Lord, hear us
and help us to serve you.

We ask your blessing
upon all who are finding life difficult
through illness or oppression.
We pray for all who feel their abilities
are being wasted or thwarted
through illness or circumstance.
May we know that in whatever circumstance
we find ourselves
God still loves us and calls us to love him.

Silence

Lord, hear us
and help us to serve you.

We rejoice that we are called to life eternal.
We remember friends and loved ones
who are departed from us.
May we all share in your abiding love
and the fullness of life eternal.

Silence

Merciful Father,
accept these prayers
for the sake of your Son,
our Saviour Jesus Christ.
Amen.

29 Reflecting God's love

Blessed are you, Lord God, King of the Universe,
for you have created us in your own image.
You have called us to reflect your love
and your forgiveness to all.
Blessed are you, Father, Son and Holy Spirit.

We pray that your Church may reflect
your love and your mercy;
that we may live as those who share
your peace and your forgiveness;
that we may seek to live in harmony and peace
with each other;
that we will be known as Christians by our love.

Silence

Living and loving God,
hear us and help us.

We ask your blessing upon all who are suffering
from acts of violence and war at this time.
We remember all who are suffering
through the anger and hatred of others.
Lord, may they not be overcome with evil
but overcome evil with good.
We pray for the work of the United Nations
and all peacekeeping forces.

Silence

Living and loving God,
hear us and help us.

Lord, we thank you
for all who have shown us the way of love
through their own self-giving and generosity.
We ask your blessing upon our homes
and all who are dear to us.
We remember before you
all who are denied human love
or who feel rejected at this time.

Silence

Living and loving God,
hear us and help us.

We remember all whose lives are being destroyed
by hatred and resentment,
all who are caught up in violence and war.
We pray for all who are suffering in our world,
especially those who feel they are on their own
without help.
We ask your blessing upon all who work
for the relief of suffering and sorrow.

Silence

Living and loving God,
hear us and help us.

We rejoice in the fellowship of your saints
and all who have reflected your image here on earth.
We pray for friends and loved ones
who have enriched our lives
and are now departed from us.
Lord, we commit ourselves, all on earth and in heaven
to you and your unfailing love.

Silence

Merciful Father,
accept these prayers
for the sake of your Son,
our Saviour Jesus Christ.
Amen.

30 Renew your people

Blessed are you, Lord our God,
who sent your Son to be our Saviour.
In your love you have opened for us
the way to eternal life
and rescued us from perishing.
Blessed are you, Father, Son and Holy Spirit.

Come, Lord, to refresh and renew your Church,
which without you is dull and dry.
Come fill the Church,
which without you is dead.
Fill the Church with your life-giving presence
and give it the power
to proclaim the resurrection to eternal life.
Lord, renew our faith in you.
Give to your Church a new sense of mission and outreach.
Bless all preachers and ministers of the sacraments
with the joy of the Good News.

Silence

Come, Lord, revive us,
renew your people.

Come, Lord, be known
in all who share in your saving purpose.
Guide and bless all rescue workers.
We remember doctors and nurses,
ambulance workers and paramedics.
We pray for the fire service, the people on lifeboats
and all who risk their lives
in the care and service of others.
We pray for all who are carers within our communities.

Silence

Come, Lord, revive us,
renew your people.

Come, Lord, let your presence be known
in our homes and in our lives.
Bless us in all our relationships
and dealings with others.
Come, Lord, with your light and love
to lives that are struggling with poverty and debt,
with bad housing and broken-down communities.

Silence

Come, Lord, revive us,
renew your people.

Come, Lord, to all whose hope is gone,
the lost, the despairing and the deeply depressed.
We remember the over-worked, the world-weary,
the exhausted and the worn-out.
We ask your blessing
upon those who feel wrung out and dry,
all who feel numb
and those whose senses are deadened.
We pray for all suffering from deep stress or trauma
and their loved ones caring for them.

Silence

Come, Lord, revive us,
renew your people.

We give thanks for the hope of life eternal.
We remember in your presence
our friends and loved ones departed.
May we all come to know the joys of your kingdom
and the fullness of life eternal.

Silence

Merciful Father,
accept these prayers
for the sake of your Son,
our Saviour Jesus Christ.
Amen.

31 Servants of love

Blessed are you, Lord our God,
for you love us with an everlasting love.
We rejoice that nothing can separate us
from your love in Christ Jesus.
Lord, help us to show your love to each other
at all times.
Blessed are you, Father, Son and Holy Spirit.

Loving God, we give thanks
for the fellowship of the Church
and for all who have taught us the faith.
We pray for preachers and teachers,
for evangelists and Bible translators.
We ask your blessing upon all Sunday schools,
study groups and those who are learning to pray.
We remember all who are seeking to grow
in love of you and in faith.

Silence

God of love,
hear us and help us.

Loving God, we give thanks
for all who reveal your love and care
through dedicated lives.
We ask your blessing upon all those who work
among the deprived and underprivileged peoples
of the world.
We remember all who seek to bring peace and unity
to communities and nations.
We pray for all who are homeless and in need.

Silence

God of love,
hear us and help us.

Loving God, we give thanks
for all who have shown us love and care.
We ask your blessing upon our homes and loved ones.
We remember all who are separated from their loved ones
through illness or circumstance.
We pray especially for the lonely
and any who feel unloved.

Silence

God of love,
hear us and help us.

Loving God, we thank you
for all who reveal love
through working in the healing professions.
We pray for doctors and nurses
and remember our own doctors and hospitals.
We ask your blessing upon all who are ill or suffering,
especially those who have no one to care for them.

Silence

God of love,
hear us and help us.

Loving God, we give you thanks
for the gift of eternal life.
We rejoice in the fellowship of all your saints
and ask your blessing upon all our loved ones departed.
May we share with them
in the fullness and glory of your kingdom.

Silence

Merciful Father,
accept these prayers
for the sake of your Son,
our Saviour Jesus Christ.
Amen.

32 Using God's gifts

Blessed are you, Lord our God,
for you have given us all talents and abilities.
You have created each of us in a unique way,
that we may give our own unique service and talents to you.
Blessed are you, Father, Son and Holy Spirit.

Lord, giver of all good gifts,
we give you thanks for all you have given us.
May we share our talents and use them
to the benefit of others and for your glory.
We pray today for all who tell others of your love
and proclaim the Gospel.
We ask your blessing upon all who minister to others.

Silence

Giver of all good gifts,
hear us and help us to live to your glory.

Lord, giver of all good gifts,
we ask your blessing upon all artists, musicians, craftspeople,
gardeners, architects, politicians
and all who use their gifts to improve our world.
We remember all who are unable
to use their talents to the full
through oppression or other circumstance.

Silence

Giver of all good gifts,
hear us and help us to live to your glory.

Lord, giver of all good gifts,
bless us and our loved ones.
We pray that our homes may be places
where talent is fostered
and given the chance to grow.
We ask your blessing upon all schools and places of learning
and all who help others to develop skills.

Silence

Giver of all good gifts,
hear us and help us to live to your glory.

Lord, giver of all good gifts,
bless all who are thwarted in their ability
through illness, oppression or the lack of opportunity.
We pray for all who are struggling
due to poverty and hunger.
We remember before you loved ones and friends who are ill.

Silence

Giver of all good gifts,
hear us and help us to live to your glory.

Lord, giver of all good gifts,
we thank you for the gift of life eternal.
We rejoice in the fellowship of all your saints
and ask your blessing on our loved ones departed,
that they may be at home with you
in your kingdom of love.

Silence

Merciful Father,
accept these prayers
for the sake of your Son,
our Saviour Jesus Christ.
Amen.

33 God's blessings

Blessed are you, Lord our God,
for you come to us
and seek to make your home with us.
Let our doors and our ears be open to you.
Let our hearts find their rest and their joy in you,
that we may grow in grace and live to your glory.
Blessed are you, Father, Son and Holy Spirit.

We ask your blessing upon all who proclaim the Good News.
We pray for preachers and evangelists,
for teachers in schools and Sunday schools.
We remember all at theological colleges.
May we hear and receive your word,
that it may grow in us and that we may serve you.
We pray for all who have never heard
or who have closed their minds to the Gospel.

Silence

Loving God,
hear us and help us.

We give thanks for the harvests of our world
and for all who provide us with food and our needs.
We pray for farmers and all who work in agriculture.
We ask your blessing upon all who suffer from a bad harvest.
We remember the world's poor and the hungry.
We ask your guidance upon all who work for Fair Trade.

Silence

Loving God,
hear us and help us.

We give thanks for our homes
and pray that you will always be at home
in our homes and our hearts.
We pray for the young who are growing in the faith
and for their nurture.
May we all make room
in our lives and in our days
to know you and your love.
We remember all who are struggling
with their relationships
and pray for all who have hardened their hearts.

Silence

Loving God,
hear us and help us.

We ask your guidance upon all who are caught up
in the cares of this world,
who are overwrought and anxious.
We remember those who are fearful of what the future holds,
for all who are lost in materialism
and know no standards but those of wealth.
We pray for all who have become poor in spirit.
We ask your blessing upon all who are ill or suffering
and their loved ones who care for them.

Silence

Loving God,
hear us and help us.

We give thanks for your saints in glory
and pray that our loved ones departed
may know the joy of your kingdom.
We commend this world, our families and ourselves
to your unfailing love.

Silence

Merciful Father,
accept these prayers
for the sake of your Son,
our Saviour Jesus Christ.
Amen.

34 Caring for God's world

Blessed are you, Lord our God,
for you have given us a world full of beauty and wonder
and have created us in your image.
Yet we have abused the world and marred your image.
Lord, in your goodness, heal your world and restore us.
Blessed are you, Father, Son and Holy Spirit.

We give thanks
that you have called us to work for you.
Through your Spirit
give us the gifts of wisdom and love in all our dealings.
We ask your blessing upon the Church
where it is working among the oppressed
and rejected peoples of our world.
Give your Church courage to stand against evil
and work for the good of all.

Silence

Lord, guide us
and help us.

We give thanks
for the balance and harmony of your creation.
We pray for all who are working to stop pollution
of land, sea and air;
all who work to protect
the species and the harvests of our world.
We ask your blessing upon those
who seek to care for the rain forests.
We pray for all who strive for justice
and for the social welfare of all people.

Silence

Lord, guide us
and help us.

We give thanks
for our loved ones and our homes
and ask you to bless and protect us.
We remember all who are forced to live
in slums or shantytowns
and those who live on the streets of our cities.
We pray for all whose relationships have broken down,
especially those full of anger or guilt.

Silence

Lord, guide us
and help us.

We pray for all who have suffered
through the wickedness or evil of others.
We remember victims of crime, violence and abuse.
We pray for all whose memories are scarred.
We ask your blessing on households that have suffered
because one member has gone astray.
We pray for all who are ill and in need of care.

Silence

Lord, guide us
and help us.

We give thanks that you are a loving and forgiving God;
in you we can be healed, restored and renewed.
We ask you to bless our loved ones departed,
that they may know and rejoice in your love.
We commit ourselves and all of creation
to your saving power and love.

Silence

Merciful Father,
accept these prayers
for the sake of your Son,
our Saviour Jesus Christ.
Amen.

35 Harvest

Blessed are you, Lord our God,
for you have given us a good earth
and a wonderful life.
May we use the resources of the earth aright
to respect all of creation,
relieve the needs of the poor
and give you glory.
Blessed are you, Father, Son and Holy Spirit.

Creating and loving God,
we thank you for the beauty and balance of our world.
We give glory to you for the mystery and wonders of creation.
May your Church help to witness
that the world belongs to you.
We pray for all who seek to proclaim the Good News
in areas of deprivation or opposition.
We ask your blessing upon all who preach the word
and all who do so by their example.

Silence

Gracious God, in your goodness,
hear us and help us.

Creating and loving God,
we ask you to bless with wisdom
all who are employers
and all who direct multinational companies.
May they not abuse or treat their workforce with injustice.
We pray for all who seek to bring about fair trade.
We remember also all who are unemployed
or do not have enough resources for healthy living.

Silence

Gracious God, in your goodness,
hear us and help us.

Creating and loving God,
we thank you for our homes and loved ones.
Help us to respect all who work
to supply us with our needs.
We pray for all who work
in the farming and retail industries.
May we always be aware that all good comes from you.
We ask your blessing upon all who are homeless
and all who feel they are not loved.

Silence

Gracious God, in your goodness,
hear us and help us.

Creating and loving God,
we remember all ill and suffering people.
We pray for those who are struggling to survive
and all who are oppressed by war, violence and tyranny.
We ask your blessing upon all who have been injured
or who have suffered from acts of violence.

Silence

Gracious God, in your goodness,
hear us and help us.

Creating and loving God,
you give us all that we have
and you offer us life eternal.
We rejoice in the fellowship of all your saints
and we commend our loved ones departed,
the whole of your creation and ourselves
to your unfailing love.

Silence

Merciful Father,
accept these prayers
for the sake of your Son,
our Saviour Jesus Christ.
Amen.

36 Maker of heaven and earth

Blessed are you, Lord our God.
All things come from you
and of your own do we give you.
From you come our life, this world
and all that we have and are.
Teach us to love and respect your creation
and give glory to you.
Blessed are you, Father, Son and Holy Spirit.

Lord God, Creator of all, we give thanks
for those who have taught us the faith.
We ask your blessing upon the mission of the Church,
which is your mission.
Guide and strengthen all who reach out to others
in faith and with the Good News.
We pray for all evangelists
and all who witness to your love.

Silence

Lord God, maker of heaven and earth,
in your love hear us.

Lord God, Creator of all, we give thanks
for all you have given us.
We ask your guidance on all who are led astray
by the glitter of gold
and the false promises of consumerism.
We pray for all who are impoverished in spirit.
We ask your blessing
upon the governments of the world
and their striving for justice and fair dealing.

Silence

Lord God, maker of heaven and earth,
in your love hear us.

Lord God, Creator of all, we ask your blessing
upon our home and our loved ones.
We pray for all who provide us
with water, electricity and gas,
for those who collect our refuse and clean our streets.
We remember all who help to maintain law and order.

Silence

Lord God, maker of heaven and earth,
in your love hear us.

Lord God, Creator of all, we ask your blessing
upon all hospitals, care homes,
home visitors and the social services.
We remember before you
all suffering and impoverished peoples.
We pray for the world's poor
and all who are without the basic needs of life.
We bring before you friends and loved ones who are ill.

Silence

Lord God, maker of heaven and earth,
in your love hear us.

Lord God, Creator of all, we come from you
and we return to you.
Bless our loved ones departed.
May they rejoice with your saints in glory.
We commit this world and ourselves
to you and your unfailing love.

Silence

Merciful Father,
accept these prayers
for the sake of your Son,
our Saviour Jesus Christ.
Amen.

37 Trusting God

Blessed are you, Lord God,
for you are our Creator and Redeemer;
you are our Strength and Shield.
As you love us with an everlasting love
and offer us life eternal,
help us to trust in you and in your grace.
Blessed are you, Father, Son and Holy Spirit.

Lord, help us to love the world
with the great love that you have for the world.
Guide your Church, that it may keep its priorities
and that above all it may seek you and your will
in all that it does.
Lord, increase our faith in you,
that we may reveal your presence in our lives.
We ask your blessing
upon all who are suffering for their beliefs
or who are struggling with their faith.

Silence

Lord God, hear us:
help us to put our trust in you.

Father, we thank you for the beauty of the earth,
for flowers and birds.
We pray for all who seek to conserve and protect
the world in which we live.
We ask your blessing upon all who deal with limited resources,
upon those who care for fish stocks,
and those who deal with the rain forests.
We pray for all who are short of food
or deprived of proper homes.

Silence

Lord God, hear us:
help us to put our trust in you.

We give thanks for our lives
and your love towards us.
Lord, bless our families and friends with your goodness.
May the way we live show our trust in you.
Let us not squander or hoard
the good things you have given us
but use them to the good and benefit of all.

Silence

Lord God, hear us:
help us to put our trust in you.

God of love and peace, we remember before you
all who are weighed down with anxiety or fear.
We pray for those who are depressed
and those who feel they can no longer cope with life.
We ask your blessing upon all who are ill
and all who suffer in any way.
May they come to know your love and your peace.

Silence

Lord God, hear us:
help us to put our trust in you.

We give thanks for your everlasting love
and we rejoice in the gift of eternal life.
Lord, we commend to you
our friends and loved ones who are departed from us.
May they enjoy your presence and your love.
We commit them, this world and ourselves
to your unfailing presence and peace.

Silence

Merciful Father,
accept these prayers
for the sake of your Son,
our Saviour Jesus Christ.
Amen.

38 Your kingdom come

Blessed are you, Lord our God.
You are our refuge and strength,
an ever-present help in trouble.
We seek to put our trust in you
and to do your will,
that your kingdom may come in us
as it is in heaven.
Blessed are you, Father, Son and Holy Spirit.

Lord God, help us to build our lives on a firm foundation:
to put our trust in you and your saving love.
Strengthen your Church when it is beset
by the storms of the world,
that it may remain firm in the faith
and obedient to you.
We pray for all who are seekers,
looking for meaning and purpose in their lives
and in the world.
We remember all who are being persecuted for their faith.

Silence

Lord, your kingdom come,
your will be done.

We ask your blessing upon all who teach and influence others,
upon those who set standards
and offer ways of living to our society.
We pray for all who are involved in government,
in broadcasting and in the press.
We remember all whose lives
have been caught up in floods, famine or war,
all who feel fragile and endangered.
We pray for all who help others to rebuild their lives.

Silence

Lord, your kingdom come,
your will be done.

We give thanks for those who have provided us
with security and protection.
We ask your blessing upon our homes and our loved ones.
We pray for the places where we work
and for those with whom we spend our leisure time.
We remember all homeless and stateless people.

Silence

Lord, your kingdom come,
your will be done.

We bring before you
all whose world has fallen apart this week.
We remember those who have lost loved ones,
who have lost freedom, employment
or who have had their homes repossessed.
We pray for all who have been involved in accidents
or who have suddenly become ill.
We ask your blessing
upon those who are close to death.

Silence

Lord, your kingdom come,
your will be done.

We ask your blessing upon our loved ones
who have departed from us –
passing through that great flood we call death.
May they rejoice in your welcome
and in your kingdom.

Silence

Merciful Father,
accept these prayers
for the sake of your Son,
our Saviour Jesus Christ.
Amen.

39 As it is in heaven

Blessed are you, Lord our God,
for you have given us of your kingdom.
You invite us to share in your Godly rule
and in the riches of life that is eternal.
Lord, teach us to seek you
until we know you and love you
and are aware of your transforming power in all the world.
Blessed are you, Father, Son and Holy Spirit.

We ask your blessing upon all who seek
to proclaim the Good News of your kingdom.
We pray for preachers of the word
and ministers of the sacraments,
for evangelists and all who witness in their daily lives
to your presence and power.
We remember those who quietly transform their surroundings
for the better
and those who show others of your kingdom in their midst.

Silence

Lord, your kingdom come,
in us as it is in heaven.

Lord we ask for the gift of discernment
in those who influence the lives of others.
We pray for all who are involved in shaping our world
through government,
through broadcasting and the press.
We ask your blessing upon all who teach
and all who are set up as examples
for our young people to follow.

Silence

Lord, your kingdom come,
in us as it is in heaven.

We give thanks for the great riches you have given us
through our home and loved ones.
May we always appreciate the care and attention
that have been shown to us.
As we have richly received, so may we share;
as we are loved, so may we love.
We pray for homes where there is tension
and a breakdown in relationships.

Silence

Lord, your kingdom come,
in us as it is in heaven.

May we not lose sight of things eternal
among all that happens in our lives.
We ask your blessing upon all who find life dull,
all who are depressed or have lost hope.
We pray for all who struggle with illness
or difficult circumstances.
We remember those who are in hospital
and all who cannot cope on their own.

Silence

Lord, your kingdom come,
in us as it is in heaven.

We give thanks for the promise
of your kingdom and life eternal.
We rejoice in the fellowship of all your saints
and commend our loved ones departed,
this world and ourselves
to your unfailing love.

Silence

Merciful Father,
accept these prayers
for the sake of your Son,
our Saviour Jesus Christ.
Amen.

40 Your will be done

Blessed are you, Lord our God,
for in your Son you have come among us
and shared in our humanity,
that we may come to you
and share in your divinity.
You have given us a wonderful Saviour
and revealed the depth of your love.
Blessed are you, Father, Son and Holy Spirit.

Lord God, we seek to do your will,
that your Church may be the instrument
of your peace and salvation.
We ask your blessing
upon all who go out in mission
and all who proclaim the Good News.
We remember especially
any who risk their lives or well-being
for the sake of doing your will.
We pray for all who seek to dedicate their lives
to you and your glory.

Silence

Lord, your will be done
on earth as in heaven.

Lord God, may your will be done
on earth as it is in heaven.
We ask your blessing upon all
who strive to bring healing and wholeness
to peoples and nations.
We pray for peacekeeping forces
and all who endeavour to maintain law and order.
We pray for the United Nations
and for our queen and government.

Silence

Lord, your will be done
on earth as in heaven.

Lord God, may we reveal your will in our homes
by living together in love and peace.
We ask your blessing upon our loved ones and friends.
May we encourage one another to do your will.
We pray for all who suffer from bad housing
or live in areas of deprivation.
We ask your blessing
upon all who seek to relieve the needs of the poor.

Silence

Lord, your will be done
on earth as in heaven.

Lord God, we pray today for all who are suffering
from strained or broken relationships.
We remember all who are a bad influence
and lead others astray.
We pray for all caught up in drugs or vice.
May they be given the chance of new directions.
We pray for friends and loved ones who are ill or in trouble.

Silence

Lord, your will be done
on earth as in heaven.

Lord God, we give thanks for our salvation
through Jesus Christ our Saviour.
Bless your saints and our loved ones departed
with the joy of your presence
and the fullness of life eternal.

Silence

Merciful Father,
accept these prayers
for the sake of your Son,
our Saviour Jesus Christ.
Amen.

41 The joy of the kingdom

Blessed are you, Lord our God,
for you have called us
to know you and to love you.
You invite us to experience the joy
of coming into your presence
and to delight in your grace.
Lord, we come
depending on your grace and goodness.
Blessed are you, Father, Son and Holy Spirit.

Good and gracious God,
may our lives show the joy of knowing you and your love.
Let preachers and teachers encourage all who hear them
to come to you in love.
Bless all who seek to extend our lives
by a vision of your grace and goodness.
We pray today for all religious writers and broadcasters.

Silence

Lord of life and love,
grant us the joy of your kingdom.

Good and gracious God,
as we go about our daily work
may we show our joy in your presence.
We ask your blessing upon all who encourage us
to relax, to be still and to be attentive.
We pray for artists and musicians,
for craftspeople and gardeners,
for all who beautify our world.
We remember all who live in deprived and derelict areas
and pray especially for the world's poor.

Silence

Lord of life and love,
grant us the joy of your kingdom.

Good and gracious God,
we thank you for the love and attention
we have received through our homes and dear ones.
We ask your blessing upon our families and friends
and the communities in which we live and work.
We remember all who strive to improve our environment.
We pray for all who are homeless
and those who live on the streets
of our towns and cities.

Silence

Lord of life and love,
grant us the joy of your kingdom.

Good and gracious God,
we thank you for our well-being.
We ask your blessing upon all who are sad or depressed
and all whose lives are darkened with troubles.
We remember all who are ill
and their loved ones as they care for them.
We pray for those who work in hospitals
and all who care for people in trouble.

Silence

Lord of life and love,
grant us the joy of your kingdom.

Good and gracious God,
you invite us all into your presence,
and to life eternal.
May we not lose sight of the eternal
through the clamour and call of the world.
We ask your blessing upon our loved ones departed.
May they rejoice with the saints in the fullness of eternal life.

Silence

Merciful Father,
accept these prayers
for the sake of your Son,
our Saviour Jesus Christ.
Amen.

42 King of Love

Blessed are you, Lord our King and our God,
for you have made us and we belong to you.
You have revealed your love for us
in the coming of Christ our Lord
and in the sending of the Holy Spirit.
Blessed are you, Father, Son and Holy Spirit.

Loving Lord, we ask your blessing
upon all who seek to care for your people.
We pray for all bishops, priests and deacons,
all who preach the word, administer the sacraments
and show pastoral care.
May we all share in your outreach and mission of love.
We remember especially those who are reaching out
to the confused and the lost.

Silence

King of Love,
Good Shepherd, hear us.

Loving Lord, we ask your blessing
upon this world, which is your creation.
We remember today all who are struggling
against evil, war or poverty.
We pray for all who share in your redeeming work
through their caring for others
and seeking to bring them freedom.
We pray for all relief agencies
and all who reach out to those in need.

Silence

King of Love,
Good Shepherd, hear us.

Loving Lord, we ask your blessing
upon our homes and our loved ones.
We remember today all who live alone
and those who are homeless.
We pray especially for young people
living on the streets of our towns and cities
and all whose lives were diminished
by circumstances they could not avoid.

Silence

King of Love,
Good Shepherd, hear us.

Loving Lord, we ask your blessing
upon all who are ill at home or in hospital.
We remember also loved ones
who are caring for them
and are anxious and fearful.
We pray for all who cannot cope on their own.
We ask your blessing upon all carers
and those involved in medical care
and the rescue services.

Silence

King of Love,
Good Shepherd, hear us.

Loving Lord, we ask your blessing
upon our friends and loved ones
who have departed from us.
May they share with your saints in glory.
To you and your loving presence
we commit this world and ourselves
and ask that we may know you
as the King of Love, our Saviour and our Friend.

Silence

Merciful Father,
accept these prayers
for the sake of your Son,
our Saviour Jesus Christ.
Amen.

43 Advent 1: Revelation

Blessed are you, Lord our God,
for you have created us out of your love
and for your love.
You have given us eyes to see,
minds to understand
and hearts to love you.
Help us to be aware of your presence
and your coming to us
this day and always.

We ask your blessing
upon all preachers and ministers of the word,
that they may proclaim your presence
and the coming of your kingdom.
We remember before you
all who seek to witness to your abiding love
and your dwelling among us.
We pray for your faithful people
as they prepare to celebrate Christmas
and to rejoice in your love for them.

Silence

Come, Lord God,
make yourself known among us.

We pray for all who watch during the darkness of night
and seek our safety.
We remember the police, coastguards, fire crews,
the ambulance service and all doctors and nurses.
We ask your blessing
upon all who work through the night
to provide us with our daily needs.

Silence

Come, Lord God,
make yourself known among us.

We give you thanks for our homes and our loved ones.
At this time of preparation for Christmas
help us to make sure we have time
for each other and for you.
We remember all who will be lonely and troubled
at this time.

Silence

Come, Lord God,
make yourself known among us.

We give thanks for our health and well-being.
We remember in your presence
all who have suddenly become ill
or been injured in accidents,
and those whose lives have been darkened
by the loss of a loved one.
We ask your blessing
upon all who are homeless or hungry
and all who fear the future.
May they know your presence
and so have courage and hope in their troubles.

Silence

Come, Lord God,
make yourself known among us.

We rejoice that you come to us
and offer us life that is eternal.
We remember in your presence
our loved ones departed and all your saints.
May we all rejoice for ever in your love.

Silence

Merciful Father,
accept these prayers
for the sake of your Son,
our Saviour Jesus Christ.
Amen.

44 Advent 2: Forgiveness

Blessed are you, Lord our God,
for you sent the prophets and John the Baptist
to prepare your way.
You have told us of your coming
and you reveal yourself to us in Jesus.
You come to each of us in power and in love.
Blessed are you, Father, Son and Holy Spirit.

Father, we give thanks
for all who tell of your love
and who proclaim your coming.
We ask your blessing upon all priests and preachers,
upon all who teach the Scriptures
and tell of your coming.
Bless all who are baptised
into your presence and power.
Lord, we ask forgiveness
when your Church misuses
the resources you have given it
and when we fail to live up to your teaching and love.

Silence

Lord, come to us:
forgive us and guide us.

We remember in your presence
the troubles and sorrows of our world.
We pray for all who are caught up in war or violence,
all who suffer from the greed and insensitivity of others.
May we not misuse or squander the earth's resources
but use them with care and for the benefit of all.
We ask your blessing upon all leaders and politicians.

Silence

Lord, come to us:
forgive us and guide us.

We ask your blessing
upon all who do not look forward to Christmas.
We remember all who will be homeless or lonely
and all who are poor or deeply in debt.
We pray that our homes
may be places of love and peace
where you are welcome.
May we know that in the coming of others to us
you also come and seek our love.

Silence

Lord, come to us:
forgive us and guide us.

We remember all who are ill
and suffering at this time,
all who are distressed
and those who are overburdened.
May they know your peace and your presence.
May all who walk in darkness
come to know your light and your love.
We pray for all who are in hospital
or in care at this time.

Silence

Lord, come to us:
forgive us and guide us.

We remember all our loved ones departed,
and we pray for any who have died recently.
May they rejoice in the fullness of life
and be with you in glory.

Silence

Merciful Father,
accept these prayers
for the sake of your Son,
our Saviour Jesus Christ.
Amen.

45 Advent 3: Hope

Blessed are you, Lord our God,
who has promised us your salvation
through the prophets,
and that in you we will find healing and peace.
We come to you,
for in our coming we turn away from the darkness
and enter into the light of your presence and your love.

Mighty God and Saviour,
we pray for your Church throughout the world,
that it may witness to you
not only in word but also in deed.
May the Church reflect your love for the world
and show your acceptance and forgiveness
for all peoples.
We remember at this time
all who are persecuted for their faith
and all who are prisoners of conscience.

Silence

Come, Lord,
for our hope is in you.

We remember in your presence
all who are oppressed by tyranny or evil.
We pray for those
who have been driven out of their homes
and who have been separated from loved ones.
We ask your blessing
on all who suffer from poverty or hunger
and all who are caught up in war
or live in fear of terrorism.

Silence

Come, Lord,
for our hope is in you.

We give thanks for those who have taught us the faith
by the example of the way they live.
May we be a good example to others.
Lord, bless our homes and our loved ones
with the light of your presence.
We remember all who are struggling in their relationships
and those whose minds are full of doubt.

Silence

Come, Lord,
for our hope is in you.

Lord, we come to you for renewal and healing,
for strength and for light.
We ask your blessing
upon all who suffer from a disability
or who are ill at this time.
We remember those who are blind, lame or deaf
and those who suffer from leprosy.
We pray for all who have lost loved ones this week
and for those who are caring for the terminally ill.

Silence

Come, Lord,
for our hope is in you.

We give thanks for your renewing powers
and that you give us life and life eternal.
We remember friends and loved ones
who are departed from us.
May they rejoice in fullness of life
and in the glory of your presence.

Silence

Merciful Father,
accept these prayers
for the sake of your Son,
our Saviour Jesus Christ.
Amen.

46 Advent 4: God with us

Blessed are you, Lord our God,
for in your love you wait on us.
You trust us with your plans
and allow us to share
in the bringing in of your kingdom.
Help us at all times to trust in you
and to seek to do your will.
Blessed are you, Father, Son and Holy Spirit.

Lord, ever with us, help your Church
to proclaim your presence and your saving power.
May we seek to do your will
and help to bring in your kingdom.
As we give thanks for Joseph,
we give thanks for all men and women of vision
and all who have dedicated their lives in your service.
We ask your blessing upon all preachers
and ministers of the sacraments.
Guide all who serve you quietly in their daily lives.
We remember especially
all who struggle to serve you
while surrounded by difficult circumstances
and opposition.

Silence

God, come among us:
make your home with us.

God of freedom,
we pray for all who are oppressed.
We ask your blessing upon all who suffer
through tyranny or terrorism.
We remember all whose freedom has been diminished
through war or violence.
We pray for the poor, the hungry and the homeless.

Silence

God, come among us:
make your home with us.

We give thanks for our homes
and for all who love us.
May we show your presence in our daily living.
We pray for homes where there is neglect or lack of love,
where there is cruelty or deep selfishness.
We remember all who live alone
and those who are lonely.

Silence

God, come among us:
make your home with us.

Lord, you are with us even when it is dark.
We ask your blessing
upon all who are in pain or in fear.
We pray for those who are ill at home or in hospital
and all who have been injured this week.
We remember those who feel life has little meaning
and those who have lost their way
or who are anxious about their future.

Silence

God, come among us:
make your home with us.

We give thanks that in you life is eternal
and we ask your blessing
upon our friends and loved ones
who are departed from us.

Silence

Merciful Father,
accept these prayers
for the sake of your Son,
our Saviour Jesus Christ.
Amen.

47 Christmas: the Saviour comes

Blessed are you, Lord our God,
for in Jesus Christ, the Word made flesh,
you share in our humanity.
You come among us to be one with us
and that we may come to you.
Blessed are you, Father, Son and Holy Spirit.

Lord God, we welcome you
into our hearts, our homes, our lives.
We ask your blessing upon the Church
as it worships you throughout the world.
May it ever witness to your presence and your love.
Guide all preachers of the word
and ministers of the sacraments,
that they may lead us to you
and help us to know you and to love you.

Silence

Lord, come to us.
Save us and help us, O Lord.

We rejoice with the shepherds
and pray for peace on earth and goodwill
among all peoples.
We ask your blessing upon all areas
where there is war, conflict and oppression.
We remember those who are not at peace
with themselves or with others.
We pray for all who are disturbed or distressed.

Silence

Lord, come to us.
Save us and help us, O Lord.

Lord, born into an ordinary home, come to our homes,
that they may reflect your peace and your glory.
We ask your blessing upon all our loved ones,
those with whom we share this Christmas
and those who are not able to be with us.

Silence

Lord, come to us.
Save us and help us, O Lord.

We remember all who find this a stressful time.
We pray for the world's poor
and those who are deeply in debt.
We remember before you the homeless
and we pray for the work of Shelter
and other relief organisations.
We seek your blessing upon all who are lonely
and those who feel neglected or forgotten at this time.
We remember also all who are ill and in hospital.

Silence

Lord, come to us.
Save us and help us, O Lord.

Lord, we rejoice that you came down to earth as a human,
that we might share in the joys of the kingdom of heaven.
We remember before you friends and loved ones departed,
especially those who have died this year.
We rejoice in the fellowship of Mary and Joseph
and all your saints.
May we share with them in your glory.

Silence

Merciful Father,
accept these prayers
for the sake of your Son,
our Saviour Jesus Christ.
Amen.

48 Christmas: Holy God

Blessed are you, Lord God,
Creator of heaven and earth.
In you and in your love
heaven and earth are one.
You have sent your Son, our Saviour,
to lead us back into your kingdom.
You have called us to work with you
and have given us of your Spirit.
Blessed are you, Father, Son and Holy Spirit.

We give you thanks and praise
that we may share in your kingdom here on earth
and that in Jesus Christ
we see our humanity and your divinity as one.
We ask your blessing upon all preachers of the word,
on all who proclaim your presence
by their actions and their love.
We pray for all who are seekers
and that we may know you better and love you more.
We remember all who are being prepared
for baptism or confirmation
and all who are seeking
to commit their lives to you in love.

Silence

Holy God, come among us:
hear us and help us.

We pray for peace on earth and goodwill among all people.
We ask your blessing upon all who strive for justice and peace.
We pray for the United Nations
and all who seek to bring unity and fellowship
between nations.

Silence

Holy God, come among us:
hear us and help us.

We give thanks that Jesus was born into an earthly home
and shared in our daily life.
May we know that our homes and loved ones
are part of your kingdom.
We ask your blessing on homes
where there is strife and division, deceit and distrust.

Silence

Holy God, come among us:
hear us and help us.

We give thanks that nothing can separate us
from your love.
We ask your blessing upon all
who are ill, lonely or oppressed.
We remember friends and loved ones
who are in hospital or ill at home
and all who are caring for them.
We pray also for all who despair,
all who have lost hope or any vision of your love.

Silence

Holy God, come among us:
hear us and help us.

Loving God, you invite us to delight in your presence
and to live in your kingdom.
Lord, keep us in life eternal.
We give thanks for your faithful ones departed
and we rejoice in the fellowship of all your saints.

Silence

Merciful Father,
accept these prayers
for the sake of your Son,
our Saviour Jesus Christ.
Amen.

49 Epiphany: Seeking God

Blessed are you, Lord our God,
for you have called us to seek you,
to know and to love you.
You have revealed yourself in Jesus Christ,
our Saviour and our God.
We come to worship you.
Blessed are you, Father, Son and Holy Spirit.

We give thanks for the wise men
and the leading of a star.
We ask your blessing upon all who are seekers
and all who dedicate their lives to you.
We remember all those who lead worship
and teach of your love and salvation.
We pray today especially for the Churches of the Far East.

Silence

Lord, we seek you and call upon you:
hear us and help us.

As the wise men sought a king, we rejoice
that you are the King of kings and Lord of lords.
May your love and your will rule in our hearts.
We ask your blessing upon all leaders of people
and all who make important decisions for our world.
We pray today for all research scientists.

Silence

Lord, we seek you and call upon you:
hear us and help us.

As the Holy Family shared in an ordinary home,
we ask your blessing upon our homes.
May our homes reveal your presence
and our relationships increase our love for you.
We remember all homeless peoples,
all refugees and those who belong to homes
where there is violence or lack of love.

Silence

Lord, we seek you and call upon you:
hear us and help us.

With the gift of myrrh
there was an offering of the sorrows of our world.
We remember all who long for freedom and redemption.
We pray for all suffering people,
all who are distressed
and all who feel that no one cares for them.
We pray for the work of doctors, nurses, paramedics
and all who are involved in healing.

Silence

Lord, we seek you and call upon you:
hear us and help us.

We rejoice with Mary and Joseph,
with the shepherds and the angels,
with the wise men,
with the Church in heaven and on earth.
We commend ourselves, all peoples and the whole world
to your unfailing love.

Silence

Merciful Father,
accept these prayers
for the sake of your Son,
our Saviour Jesus Christ.
Amen.

50 New Year

Blessed are you, Lord our God,
for you are our Maker, our Saviour and our Guide.
Keep us mindful of your presence,
your love and your power,
that we may learn to rejoice in you and your love.
Blessed are you, Father, Son and Holy Spirit.

We remember before you all who are being prepared
for baptism or confirmation.
We ask your blessing upon all who seek to reveal
your love and your peace.
We pray for all preachers of the word
and all who reach out in mission.
We pray that the Church may share in your mission to the world.
Lord, help us all to reveal your glory in our midst.

Silence

Holy Trinity,
hear us and help us.

We ask your blessing upon all who are beginning
new ventures and new work.
We pray for all who are being asked to extend themselves
through learning and the development of their abilities.
We remember those who are entering into new relationships
and we ask your blessing upon those who are newly married.

Silence

Holy Trinity,
hear us and help us.

We thank you for our homes and our loved ones.
We ask your blessing upon those who are moving to a new home
or who are moving away from their families.
We remember all who are homeless,
all who live in poverty or hunger.
We pray to you for all who work
to relieve the needs and suffering of others.

Silence

Holy Trinity,
hear us and help us.

We remember before you
all who feel confused or troubled at this time.
We pray for all who are distressed
and those who are not able to cope
with what is happening around them.
May they know your presence and your power.
We ask your blessing upon all who are ill
at home or in hospital,
especially those who are fearful or lonely.

Silence

Holy Trinity,
hear us and help us.

We rejoice in the gift of life and life eternal.
We ask your blessing upon our loved ones and friends
who have departed from us.
We remember especially today
those who have enriched our lives
by their example and goodness.
May they rejoice in glory
and may we share with them in your eternal kingdom.

Silence

Merciful Father,
accept these prayers
for the sake of your Son,
our Saviour Jesus Christ.
Amen.

51 Mothering Sunday

Blessed are you, Lord our God,
for you have created us all.
We are your children,
loved by you
and ever under your care and protection.
We thank you for our life, your love
and all that you give us.
Blessed are you, Father, Son and Holy Spirit.

We thank you for the Church
that tells of your love
and helps people to know you.
Loving God, bless our Church,
that it may show your love to all who come to it.
We remember especially today
any who would have liked to be here
but were not able to come.

Silence

Life-giving and loving God,
hear us and help us.

We thank you for the wonderful world
that you have given us,
for the air we breathe and for water.
We thank you for all growing things and for food.
God bless all who work hard
to provide us with what we need.
We pray especially for hungry and homeless people.

Silence

Life-giving and loving God,
hear us and help us.

We thank you God for the love of our homes.
Thank you for the love and care of our mother.
We pray for families where a loved one is ill
or causing trouble.
We remember all who are suffering from lack of love,
and those who live in homes where there is tension
and broken relationships.

Silence

Life-giving and loving God,
hear us and help us.

We thank you for the confidence and joy we have
through knowing we are loved.
We ask your blessing
upon all who are lonely or neglected.
We pray for those separated from their loved ones
through illness or circumstance.
We pray for all who have been taken into care.

Silence

Life-giving and loving God,
hear us and help us.

We give thanks for your eternal love
and we pray to you for all our loved ones departed.
We remember all who have enriched our lives
by their goodness.
We commit our loved ones and all people
to your unfailing love.

Silence

Merciful Father,
accept these prayers
for the sake of your Son,
our Saviour Jesus Christ.
Amen.

52 Palm Sunday

Blessed are you, Lord God of our salvation;
to you be praise and glory for ever.
As we rejoice this day
in the triumphant entry into Jerusalem,
may we too be willing to walk the way of the cross.
By our lives may we witness to you as our Lord and King
and declare your saving love to the world.
Blessed are you, Father, Son and Holy Spirit.

Come, Lord.
Cleanse your Church from any pride or greed.
Cleanse us from our sins and free us to serve you.
Strengthen our sense of mission and service.
Strengthen our sensitivity towards the needs of others.
Strengthen our faith and our vision for your world.

Silence

Saviour of the world, our Redeemer,
save us and help us.

Come, Lord.
Guide the nations into the ways of justice and peace.
Guide all leaders and rulers to care for our world.
Comfort all who are broken by war and violence.
Comfort all who are shattered
by the betrayal of loved ones;
all who feel scorned and rejected.
Comfort all who are imprisoned and wrongly sentenced.

Silence

Saviour of the world, our Redeemer,
save us and help us.

Come, Lord.
As our Saviour and Friend,
bless our homes and our loved ones with your love.
Guide us in all our dealings
and help us to live with you as our Lord.
Let your kingly rule be known in us
as it is in heaven.

Silence

Saviour of the world, our Redeemer,
save us and help us.

Come, Lord.
You were broken on the cross to make us whole.
Be with all who are suffering at this time.
Come as light to those who walk in darkness,
the despairing and the despondent.
Come as joy to all who have lost confidence
and to all who are depressed.
Come as hope to all who are ill
and fearful of their future.

Silence

Saviour of the world, our Redeemer,
save us and help us.

Lord Jesus, we remember that you died
that we might live.
You descended into the depths
to raise us to the heights.
We ask your blessing
upon all our loved ones departed.
May they rejoice in the fullness of your kingdom.

Silence

Merciful Father,
accept these prayers
for the sake of your Son,
our Saviour Jesus Christ.
Amen.

53 Easter Day: Risen Lord

Blessed are you, Lord God,
by whose power our Lord Jesus is raised from the dead.
In your presence is life and life eternal.
In your power death is conquered
and the gate to eternal life is opened.
In your presence is the fullness of joy.
Blessed are you, Father, Son and Holy Spirit.

Lord, make us aware of your risen presence in our lives.
May our worship be full of joy and awe.
Give us the courage to go out
to proclaim your love and your saving power.
Lord, as we celebrate your resurrection,
strengthen your Church
to tell the Good News to the whole world.
Bless all who are called to teach and preach in your name.
In the power of the risen Lord,
may they lead us from darkness to his glorious light.

Silence

Risen Lord,
deliver us from the dominion
of darkness and death.

Lord Jesus, as we rejoice in your risen presence,
we pray that the world may know your peace.
May we rise above division and strife,
that your victory over darkness and death
may be known in the world.
Lord, show us the peace we should give,
the peace we should share
and the peace we must forgo.

Silence

Risen Lord,
deliver us from the dominion
of darkness and death.

Risen Lord, you appeared to the two Marys
and sent them to tell the disciples.
Help us to show your presence in our homes
and in all our dealings.
Let us walk and work in your presence
and seek to reveal your glory in the world.
We ask you to bless all our loved ones and friends
and keep us ever in your love.

Silence

Risen Lord,
deliver us from the dominion
of darkness and death.

We remember all who walk in darkness
and who are heavily burdened.
We pray for all who have lost hope and who despair.
We ask your blessing upon all who are chronically ill
and those who can no longer cope on their own.
We pray for all who are approaching death
and their loved ones who are caring for them.

Silence

Risen Lord,
deliver us from the dominion
of darkness and death.

Risen Lord, we ask that we might share in your resurrection
and triumph over darkness and death.
We ask your blessing upon our friends and loved ones
who are departed from us.
May they have a share with your saints in glory.
This day we rejoice that death is conquered:
we are free, for Christ has won the victory.

Silence

Merciful Father,
accept these prayers
for the sake of your Son,
our Saviour Jesus Christ.
Amen.

54 Easter 2: The Lord is here

Blessed are you,
God and Father of our Lord Jesus Christ.
To you be glory and praise for ever.
By raising your Son from the dead,
death has been destroyed
and new life has been restored.
In him the victory over sin and the grave is won.
As you call us to newness of life,
may our lives reflect his glory.
Blessed are you, Father, Son and Holy Spirit.

Lord, bless your Church,
that it may reveal your presence
and the power of the resurrection.
May each church community
show signs of new life and joy in you.
Through our relationship with you
may we bring others to be faithful.
We ask your blessing upon all who are seekers,
all who are new in the faith
and all who are struggling
with doubt and darkness.

Silence

Lord, be known among us;
make haste to help us.

Lord, bless the world with your peace,
the peace that it cannot achieve on its own.
We pray for peace between nations and peoples.
We ask your blessing upon all peacemakers
and the work of the United Nations.
We pray for all who live in fear for their lives
and all who have lost confidence in themselves
or the world around them.

Silence

Lord, be known among us;
make haste to help us.

Lord, bless our homes and families
with the joy of your presence.
May our homes be ever open to you and your love.
We remember today all who suffer
from poverty or homelessness.
We ask your blessing upon all
who live amid strife and fear
and all who are unable to rejoice in life.

Silence

Lord, be known among us;
make haste to help us.

Lord, bless all who feel restricted
by what is happening around them.
We remember all who live in violent or deprived areas.
We ask your blessing upon all who are ill
or who have been injured through accidents,
and upon those who care for them.
Lord, give them courage and hope in their troubles.

Silence

Lord, be known among us;
make haste to help us.

Lord of life and life eternal,
bless our loved ones departed,
that in fellowship with all your saints
they may rejoice in the fullness
of your presence and glory.

Silence

Merciful Father,
accept these prayers
for the sake of your Son,
our Saviour Jesus Christ.
Amen.

55 Ascension: King of kings

Blessed are you, Lord our God,
for in the ascension of your Son
you have raised us on high
and given us a glimpse of eternal life
and the promise of your abiding presence.
Blessed are you, Father, Son and Holy Spirit.

Risen and ascended Lord,
you have promised to be with us always.
Help us to rejoice in your presence
and to proclaim your saving power.
We ask your blessing upon all who preach the Good News,
all who teach from the Scriptures
and all who witness to you in their daily lives.

Silence

Ascended Lord, King of kings,
rule in our hearts and in the world.

Risen and ascended Lord,
you are the King of kings.
We pray for the time
when the kingdoms of this world
will be seen as your kingdom.
We ask your blessing upon all rulers,
leaders and politicians,
that they may be guided by your rule.
We pray for all who are in captivity
through injustice or tyranny.

Silence

Ascended Lord, King of kings,
rule in our hearts and in the world.

Risen and ascended Lord,
we rejoice that you are with us
in our homes and our daily lives.
May we be at home with you.
We remember all who live in bad housing,
squalor or deprivation.
We pray for all who have been made homeless
and for any who are suffering
from broken relationships.

Silence

Ascended Lord, King of kings,
rule in our hearts and in the world.

Risen and ascended Lord,
we remember before you all who have lost hope
and have no vision of glory.
We pray for those who live mediocre lives
and all who are caught up in crime, vice or drugs.
We ask your blessing upon all who are ill
and especially those who are nearing death.

Silence

Ascended Lord, King of kings,
rule in our hearts and in the world.

Risen and ascended Lord,
you have opened for us the gate of glory.
We rejoice in the fellowship of your saints
and the faithful departed.
As we ask your blessing
upon our loved ones departed from us,
we commit this world, each other and ourselves
to your unfailing love.

Silence

Merciful Father,
accept these prayers
for the sake of your Son,
our Saviour Jesus Christ.
Amen.

56 Ascension: With us always

Blessed are you, Lord our God,
for you have raised your Son
from the darkness of death
to the fullness of life eternal,
to your right hand on high.
By his death he has destroyed death;
by his rising to life again
he has restored to us eternal life;
by his ascension he has opened for us the gate of glory.
Blessed are you, Father, Son and Holy Spirit.

As we rejoice in the ascension,
we give thanks for men and women of vision,
for those who have shared their faith with us.
We remember all whose lives are clouded by doubt or despair.
We pray for those who feel life is dull,
that they may come to know
the joy of the presence of the ascended Lord.
Lord, empower your Church
to proclaim the Good News of your saving acts.

Silence

Lord, with us always,
hear us and help us.

As we rejoice in your presence,
we remember all who feel lonely and neglected in our world.
We ask your blessing on all who are oppressed
and those who are struggling to survive.
We pray for all who are caught up in violence and war,
and for those not at peace with each other,
with themselves and with you.

Silence

Lord, with us always,
hear us and help us.

As we rejoice in your love,
we remember our loved ones,
our homes and families.
We pray for our community and neighbourhood.
We ask your blessing
upon all who strive to brighten the world
by their dedication and goodness,
by their faith and willingness to sacrifice.

Silence

Lord, with us always,
hear us and help us.

As we rejoice in your power,
we remember all whose powers are waning,
the elderly and the infirm
and all who are disabled.
We ask your blessing upon all who are ill
or who have been injured in accidents.
May they find courage and hope in you
and in your abiding love.

Silence

Lord, with us always,
hear us and help us.

We rejoice that you are our great High Priest,
who ascended into heaven,
and that you are at the right hand of God
making intercession for us.
May our loved ones departed and all your faithful
rejoice in you and rest in the glory of your kingdom.

Silence

Merciful Father,
accept these prayers
for the sake of your Son,
our Saviour Jesus Christ.
Amen.

57 Pentecost: Holy Spirit, come

Blessed are you, Lord our God.
To you be praise and glory for ever.
As your Spirit moved over the face of the deep,
bringing life to the world,
and as the same Spirit filled the disciples at Pentecost,
come to us, refresh us and renew us.
Blessed are you, Father, Son and Holy Spirit.

Holy Spirit of God, moving in the deep of creation,
come into the depths of our lives,
guide us and empower us.
We ask your blessing upon the Church,
that it may have the courage
to proclaim the Good News and tell of your power.
May the Church be seen as Spirit-filled
through its display of the gifts of the Spirit.
Guide us, that each of us may use our gifts and talents
to your glory and the benefit of each other.

Silence

Holy Spirit of God, come:
refresh us and renew us.

Holy Spirit of God, giving life to dry bones,
we ask your blessing upon all who feel threatened
or who have lost hope.
We remember before you
refugees, homeless and oppressed peoples.
Give your strength to all who seek to bring liberty and justice.
Guide the leaders of nations
and all who are in positions of authority
into the ways of peace.

Silence

Holy Spirit of God, come:
refresh us and renew us.

Holy Spirit of God, kindle the hearts
which without you are dull and cold.
Bless us in all our relationships,
strengthen our love for each other,
give joy to us as families in our homes
and in our dealings with each other.
We pray for all who seek to restore broken relationships.

Silence

Holy Spirit of God, come:
refresh us and renew us.

Holy Spirit of God, Breath of Life,
we ask your blessing upon all who feel hindered or isolated
through illness or disability.
We remember those in constant pain
and all who are finding life difficult.
We pray for all who are despairing and depressed.

Silence

Holy Spirit of God, come:
refresh us and renew us.

Holy Spirit of God, Giver of life and life eternal,
we rejoice in your renewing and restoring power.
We ask your blessing upon our loved ones departed,
that in you they may know the fullness of life
and the joy of your presence.

Silence

Merciful Father,
accept these prayers
for the sake of your Son,
our Saviour Jesus Christ.
Amen.

58 Pentecost: Fill us with your Spirit

Blessed are you, Lord our God,
for you have made us for yourself and for your love.
We seek your presence
and desire to give our lives and our love to you.
Blessed are you, Father, Son and Holy Spirit.

Lord, may your presence be revealed
through your Church.
May we never be satisfied with words without content,
with actions without love,
with buildings that do not convey your presence.
Lord, fill us and make us a holy people,
a fulfilled people and a missionary people.
Bless the Church,
that it may grow in outreach, in holiness and in number.

Silence

Lord, we look for you; we long for you:
come fill us with your Spirit.

You have given us a wonderful world.
Let us not spoil it through greed or lack of respect.
We remember all who suffer from hunger and thirst.
We pray for all who do not have proper water supplies
or who have to walk miles to get water.
We pray also for all in the consumer society
who try to fill their lives with things
and are never satisfied.

Silence

Lord, we look for you; we long for you:
come fill us with your Spirit.

We give thanks for the longings that you have given us.
We ask your blessing upon our loved ones,
our families and friends.
We remember before you all who are lonely,
those who are failing in health or strength,
and all who are fearful for the future.

Silence

Lord, we look for you; we long for you:
come fill us with your Spirit.

We give thanks for the joy and freedom
you give to our lives.
We pray for all who have become captives
to vice and drugs,
all who are suffering from the misuse of alcohol.
We remember their families who also suffer.
We ask your blessing upon all who are ill
and upon those who care for them.

Silence

Lord, we look for you; we long for you:
come fill us with your Spirit.

In the power of your Spirit
you renew and refresh us.
We pray for all who are departed from us,
that they may rejoice in the fullness of life eternal.
To you, O God, and your love
we commit this world, our loved ones and ourselves
now and for eternity.

Silence

Merciful Father,
accept these prayers
for the sake of your Son,
our Saviour Jesus Christ.
Amen.

59 Trinity Sunday

Blessed be God, Father, Son and Holy Spirit,
the Three in One,
the holy and wonderful Trinity
bound together in one eternity of love.
Blessed be God the Creator of all things.
Blessed be the Christ, our Saviour and Friend.
Blessed be the Spirit within us, our Guide and Strength.
Blessed be God for all that he is and all he has done.
Blessed be the One and the Three.

Holy God, we ask your blessing
upon all who are baptised and confirmed in the faith,
that they may witness to your presence and love.
We pray for preachers and teachers,
that they may seek to reveal
the mystery of your being with us.
Lord, guide the mission and outreach of your people.

Silence

Holy God, Holy and Strong One,
hear us and help us.

Holy God, we give thanks for your whole creation.
Guide and bless all who work in research
and who seek to discover the mysteries of your world.
We remember all scientists and explorers.
We pray for all who are at school, college or university.
We ask your blessing upon all who provide us
with our daily needs.

Silence

Holy God, Holy and Strong One,
hear us and help us.

Holy God, be among us
in our homes and in our work.
Surround our loved ones and ourselves
with your love and protection.
We ask your blessing upon all who are recently married
and those who have a new child in their family.

Silence

Holy God, Holy and Strong One,
hear us and help us.

Holy God, you are ever ready to help us.
We ask your blessing upon all doctors, nurses
and those caring for loved ones who are ill.
We remember all ill and suffering peoples,
the poor and hungry of our world.
We pray for all who feel they are without help or hope.

Silence

Holy God, Holy and Strong One,
hear us and help us.

Holy God, giver of life and life eternal,
we rejoice in your presence
and ask your blessing upon our loved ones
who are departed from us.
May they share with your saints
in the fullness of your glorious kingdom.

Silence

Merciful Father,
accept these prayers
for the sake of your Son,
our Saviour Jesus Christ.
Amen.

60 All Saints' Day

Blessed are you, Lord our God,
for you have called us to share
in the blessedness of your saints.
Grant that in the darkness that is around us
we may be guided by their example
and so serve you in love and peace.
Blessed are you, Father, Son and Holy Spirit.

Rejoicing in the fellowship of all the saints
we pray to the Lord:

Lord, make us to be numbered with your saints
in your eternal glory.

Blessed God, we remember before you
all who have witnessed to your love and mercy.
We ask your blessing
upon all who seek to bring reconciliation and forgiveness
to peoples and communities.
We pray for all who are involved in pastoral work
and the ministry of healing.

Silence

Lord, make us to be numbered with your saints
in your eternal glory.

Blessed God, we remember before you
all who have witnessed to your peace.
We ask your blessing upon the work of the United Nations
and all peacekeeping forces.
We pray for all who are not at peace
with themselves or with the world around them
and all who suffer through war.

Silence

Lord, make us to be numbered with your saints
in your eternal glory.

Blessed God, we remember before you
all who have set us an example by their grace and goodness.
We ask your blessing upon our homes and families.
We pray for all who are suffering from broken relationships
and all who feel lonely.

Silence

Lord, make us to be numbered with your saints
in your eternal glory.

Blessed God, we remember before you
all who have suffered persecution for their faith.
We ask you to bless those who strive against injustice and evil.
We pray for all who suffer from tyranny or oppression.
We remember also all who are ill at home or in hospital,
those injured in accidents and all victims of violence.

Silence

Lord, make us to be numbered with your saints
in your eternal glory.

Blessed God, we remember before you
all the faithful departed.
We pray that our loved ones who are gone from us
may rejoice in the fellowship of all your saints in glory.

Silence

Merciful Father,
accept these prayers
for the sake of your Son,
our Saviour Jesus Christ.
Amen.

Topical Index

The numbers refer to the prayers, not the pages.
The following topics are not listed in the index because they occur in almost all the prayers:
The Church, the World, Homes and Families, the Sick, the Departed.